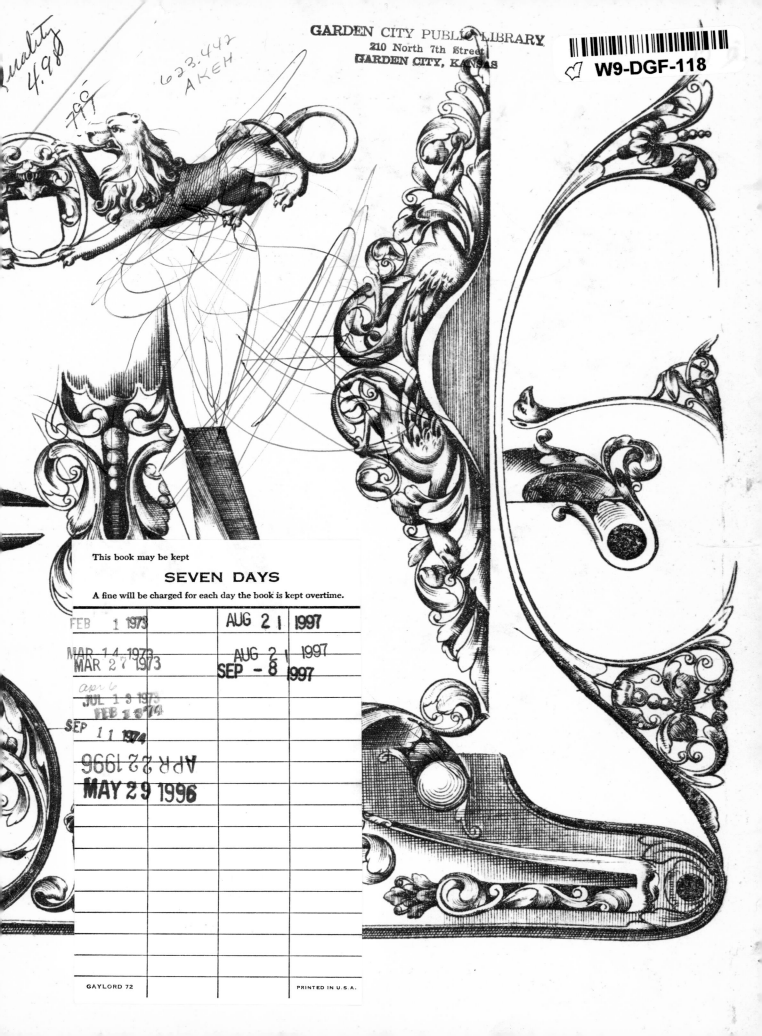

The World of Guns

The World of Guns

Richard Akehurst

HAMLYN

London · New York · Sydney · Toronto

Published by
THE HAMLYN PUBLISHING GROUP LIMITED
London · New York · Sydney · Toronto
Hamlyn House, Feltham, Middlesex, England

© Copyright The Hamlyn Publishing Group Limited 1972

ISBN 0 600 39236 8

Photoset in England by Siviter Smith Limited, Birmingham
Printed in Italy by Istituto Italiano d'Arti Grafiche,
Bergamo, Italy
Mohn Gordon Limited 1972

683
A32 gu

Contents

Endpaper:
A pattern for gun decoration from *Plusiers Models . . .*
by the Parisian gunsmiths Thuraine and le Hollandois, *c.* 1660.
Half-title:
A pattern for gun decoration by the French designer Jean Berain, from
Diverses pieces très utile par les Arquebuzières, Paris, 1659.
Title page:
A pair of over-and-under swivel-barrelled flintlock pistols by W. Bailes, London, *c.* 1750.
Contents page:
Figures from a fine engraving by Jacques Callot, *c.* 1635, showing a musketeer's drill.
The figures on the original are 20mm ($\frac{3}{4}$ inch) high.

The development of the gun

The invention of gunpowder and its use as a propellant in guns has had a profound effect upon the world. A little powder and a lead ball in an iron tube closed at one end and some means of ignition—so simple yet so deadly. From the earliest guns to those of the present the principle has remained the same.

This chapter will outline the ways in which the basic idea has been developed to make the gun more efficient. Subsequent chapters will deal with the ways in which guns have been adapted to meet particular needs and also the ways in which new inventions have changed the course of events.

There is no precise date for the invention of gunpowder. It would seem that a quick-burning substance composed of sulphur, saltpetre and charcoal was known in China and some Islamic lands before its existence was recorded in Europe. Evidence of a formula for the making of gunpowder is to be found in passages from the works of the Franciscan friar Roger Bacon written between 1250 and 1270.

It seems that the powder was at first used in various sorts of fireworks and that its possibilities as a propellant became apparent only gradually. The Chinese were the first to take up the idea and they seem to have used a bamboo tube, probably bound for extra strength, while in Europe there is evidence of the use in warfare of strange vase-like cannon in the first quarter of the fourteenth century. Early pictures of these cannon show them being ignited by a slow match held on the end of a rod, the projectile being a large iron arrow or bolt.

Once the basic principle had been established it was not long before handguns were made. The earliest consisted of an iron tube closed at the rear end and fitted to a simple wooden stock. It was ignited by some smouldering substance on the end of a short stick held in the right hand.

Crude though this method of ignition may seem, it is interesting to reflect that it continued to be the method found most satisfactory for firing cannon until the middle of the nineteenth century. However with hand weapons it was obviously a great inconvenience to have only one hand to hold the gun, while the other held the match-stick. The problem was solved by attaching an angled iron match-holder to the gun in such a way that the match was moved forward on to the priming powder when the rear end was moved up by the fingers of the right hand.

These matchlocks, fitted with what is generally described as a 'serpentine' lock, were first known to have been used in the early fifteenth century. A number of improvements followed: the barrel tube was closed at the rear end with a screwed plug, and the touch-hole was drilled into the side with a priming pan with a sliding cover set beside it. A more elaborate version of the serpentine, in which a spring was used to keep the match from the pan, was neatly recessed into the side of the stock. Gentle pressure on the lever under the stock brought the match onto the powder in the pan. This under-lever, which was liable to be moved up accidentally, was later replaced by a conventional form of trigger protected by a trigger-guard.

Forms of snap-matchlock were used in the sixteenth century, mostly for target rifles, in which the sprung match-holder was retained in position by a side-acting sear, the match springing onto the pan when released.

An early form of handgun, c. 1400, of the type usually cast in bronze. It had a wooden haft socketed in behind the breech. The gunner steadied the gun with his left hand and applied the match to the touch-hole with his right.

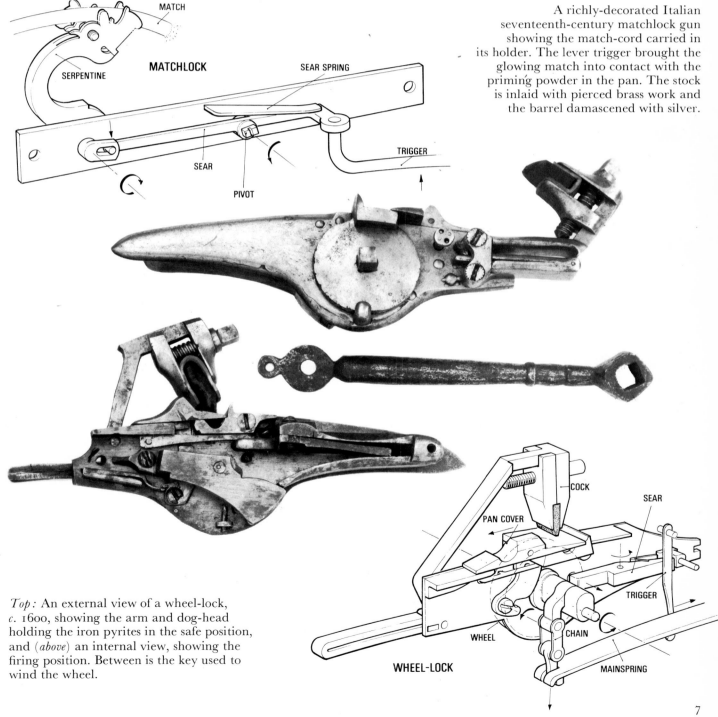

MATCHLOCK

MATCH

SERPENTINE

SEAR SPRING

TRIGGER

SEAR

PIVOT

A richly-decorated Italian
seventeenth-century matchlock gun
showing the match-cord carried in
its holder. The lever trigger brought the
glowing match into contact with the
priming powder in the pan. The stock
is inlaid with pierced brass work and
the barrel damascened with silver.

COCK

SEAR

PAN COVER

TRIGGER

WHEEL

CHAIN

MAINSPRING

WHEEL-LOCK

Top: An external view of a wheel-lock,
c. 1600, showing the arm and dog-head
holding the iron pyrites in the safe position,
and (*above*) an internal view, showing the
firing position. Between is the key used to
wind the wheel.

7

By the middle of the sixteenth century, barrels were being rifled, that is cut with spiralling grooves to impart spin to a bullet. Accuracy at a distance is gained by this device and it was used mainly in fine rifles for target shooting or in hunting guns made for the nobility.

Early matchlock guns were fitted with a wooden stock designed to be held against the cheek, the recoil being largely absorbed by the weight of the gun. However, towards the end of the sixteenth century a butt was developed that was suited to taking the recoil on the shoulder. This was particularly necessary for the more powerful military guns known as 'muskets'.

The gun, by the end of the sixteenth century, was held to the shoulder and fired by means of a trigger in a manner that has changed little since. However its ignition by smouldering match was extremely inconvenient. Whenever the gun was likely to be needed a great length of smouldering match had to be lighted and fixed in the jaws of the match-holder. This was not all: it had to be constantly moved forward as it burned back and the ash knocked off before firing. In bad weather or rough country this was obviously much more difficult to manage. The wheel-lock solved many of these problems, or rather it solved them for those who could afford this elaborate and expensive form of ignition. The common soldier and the peasant fowler however still had to rely on the match-lock.

The wheel-lock functioned in much the same manner as a cigarette lighter. On pulling the trigger, a spring-loaded wheel with a serrated edge spun rapidly, striking sparks from a piece of iron pyrites which was held upon it in a vice-like dog-head. The sparks fired the priming powder, sending a flame through the touch-hole to the main charge. The power for the wheel came from a strong V-spring which was connected to the wheel by a chain. A spanner was used to wind up the spring, and the external axis of the wheel was squared off for this purpose. The advantage of the wheel-lock was that a gun could be carried loaded and primed for instant use. Also it could be safely carried if the dog-head holding the iron pyrites was moved forward out of contact with the wheel.

There is no exact date for the invention of the wheel-lock. It seems to have been applied to guns in the early years of the sixteenth century in Germany. Leonardo da Vinci drew a type of wheel-lock in his *Codex Atlanticus* (c. 1500–5) and there is also evidence to show that the idea may have been adapted from a type of tinder lighter in use at about the same time. No doubt, when the principle of wheel-lock ignition became known, a number of gunmakers worked on its practical application. Initially they almost certainly needed the help of locksmiths or clockmakers to fashion the many intricate parts. Long after the wheel-lock had been generally superseded by the flintlock, it remained popular, particularly in Germany, for hunting and target rifles. Examples were still being made well into the eighteenth century.

The wheel-lock had had a limited distribution because of its cost. It was the relatively simple flintlock that was to supersede both the matchlock and the wheel-lock. The earliest form of flintlock was that known as the 'snaphance', which originated in Scandinavia in the middle of the sixteenth century; other versions soon appeared in various parts of Europe. The principle was that of the flint and steel tinder-

lighter. The flint was held in the jaws of the cock, which was under tension from a strong spring. The cock was pulled back until held by the sear, and on being released by the trigger it sprang downwards causing the flint to strike sparks from a steel positioned above the priming pan. As the cock moved downwards the pan cover slid clear to expose the priming to the sparks. The snaphance type of flintlock, in which the steel was separate from the pan cover, remained popular in Scandinavia, Scotland and northern Italy well into the seventeenth century. Elsewhere in Europe it was the flintlock with a combined steel and pan cover that was to become general in its distribution and to have the longest reign as the standard ignition for all types of guns.

This L-shaped combination of the steel and pan cover came into use in England and other parts of Europe in the first quarter of the seventeenth century. As a safety precaution, because the steel was in position when the pan cover was closed, a hook catch known as a 'dog' was fitted so that it hooked into a notch in the cock and held it secure. For this reason many of these early flintlocks are termed 'doglocks'. However, they were still relatively clumsy, relying on side-acting sears, and were soon replaced by the French type of lock invented in the first quarter of the seventeenth century. This French lock had a tumbler on the inside of the lock plate on a fixed axis with the cock. The mainspring bore upon this tumbler in such a manner that it was put under full tension when the cock was pulled back. There was an upright sear that slipped into two notches in the tumbler in turn as the cock was pulled back to full cock, the position for release by the trigger. If, however, the cock was to be placed in a safe position for loading or carrying, it was left at half cock, that is the sear was left in the first deep notch. This first notch was too deep for the sear to be released by the trigger; it was therefore quite safe until the cock was pulled back to full cock.

Later a bridle was added to hold the tumbler firmly in position and apart from a few minor improvements this lock was to remain standard well into the first half of the nineteenth century. The various improvements to the flintlock will mostly be dealt with in the chapter on sporting guns.

Before leaving the flintlock, an important variation should be noticed that was developed in the first half of the seventeenth century. This was the lock, found in the region of the Mediterranean, which had its origin in Spain and is sometimes called the 'miquelet' lock It was distinguished by its less graceful overall shape, its upright cock, its exterior mainspring and the side-operating sear that protruded through the face of the lock plate to catch the toe of the cock.

Satisfactory as the flintlock proved for most needs, it did have serious drawbacks. It depended on a good flint striking hot sparks into the priming. The priming was itself susceptible to damp or wet weather, and at the best there was an appreciable delay between the pulling of the trigger and the firing of the main charge.

The answer to these drawbacks was to be found in the application of detonating powders to the firing of the main charge. Detonating powders, such as gold and mercury fulminates, had been known since the seventeenth century, and disastrous experiments had been made in trying to use them in place of the main charge. The Reverend Alexander Forsyth of Belhevie in Scotland had succeeded by 1806 in using tiny

The Dutch type of snaphance lock, shown in the fired position. The cock holding the flint has struck sparks into the pan from the steel, which was flung back on its spring when struck. The sear of this lock projects through the lock plate to engage the tail end of the cock. This example dates from the second half of the sixteenth century.

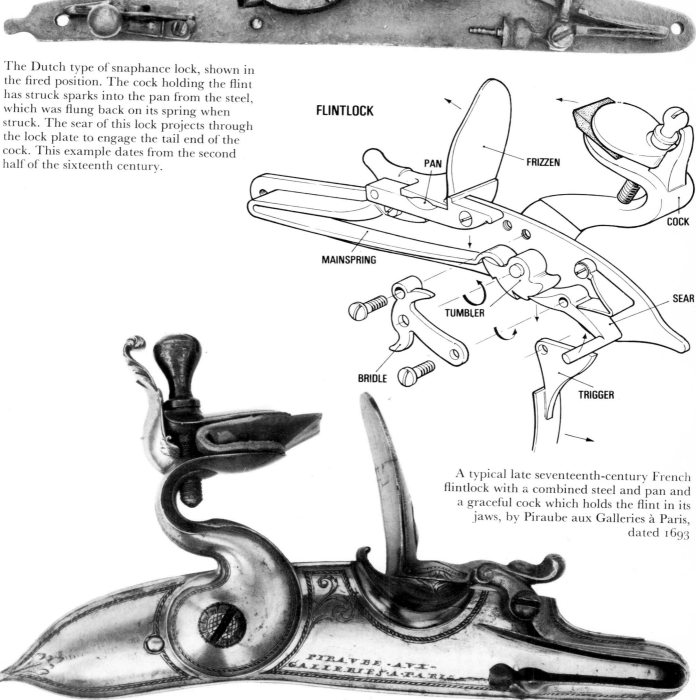

FLINTLOCK

PAN

FRIZZEN

COCK

MAINSPRING

SEAR

TUMBLER

BRIDLE

TRIGGER

A typical late seventeenth-century French flintlock with a combined steel and pan and a graceful cock which holds the flint in its jaws, by Piraube aux Galleries à Paris, dated 1693

PIRAVBE · AVX ·
GALLERIES · A · PARIS

quantities of detonating powder to fire the main charge of gunpowder. His ingenious device consisted of a small magazine fitted to the lock plate, opposite the touch-hole. On being turned a tiny quantity of powder was deposited in a cavity connected by a tube to the touch-hole. On pressing the trigger the hammer, which had replaced the cock, hit the spring-loaded firing pin, detonating the powder and sending an instantaneous flash through to the main charge. Forsyth's detonating lock was patented in 1807 but, although it worked well and moderate numbers were sold, it was expensive and required great precision of manufacture. However Forsyth's lock had shown the possibilities and it was not long before numerous variations in the use of detonating powder – in pills, discs, tapes, tubes and caps – were being tried out by other gunmakers.

By 1821, when Forsyth's patent expired, the copper percussion cap had been found to be most satisfactory. The copper cap fitted over the nipple (a steel nozzle screwed into the breech) and on being struck by the hammer it sent an instantaneous flash through the charge. As there was no appreciable delay, no priming powder to get wet or damp, and misfires were very rare, the system constituted a great improvement on the flintlock. It also created the conditions for important new advances.

The problem of muzzle-loading remained. A number of types of capping breech-loaders were developed in which a thin paper or skin cartridge was fired by an external percussion cap. However, it was a cartridge containing its own cap that was to have general application in the future. Amongst the first cartridges containing their own ignition to achieve a considerable success were the pin-fire cartridge and the needle-fire cartridge which came into use in the 1840s. The pin-fire cartridge had the percussion cap set inside and was fired by a pin which projected from the rear of the cartridge at a right angle. The needle-fire cartridge contained a detonator placed in front of the powder charge. It was fired by a long needle-like firing pin that had first to penetrate the

powder charge. A number of forms of self-contained cartridge were produced, including the rim-fire (which still has a limited use), but undoubtedly the most important was the centre-fire.

A centre-fire cartridge with a percussion cap set in the centre of a metal base was patented in France by Pottet in 1855 and Schneider patented another version in 1858. The centre-fire cartridge soon became the standard for most types of gun, rifle or pistol. The cartridge made the development of an extraordinary variety of magazine, automatic, repeating and machine guns a practical proposition.

It is interesting to note, when looking at the complexity of guns produced in the last hundred years, that the centre-fire cartridge has changed little and proved marvellously adaptable. One important change has been the replacement of gunpowder or black powder as a propellant by various nitro-compounds. Weapons likely to jam because of excessive fouling benefited enormously and smoke no longer interfered with aim.

In this brief general survey of the development of guns it is inevitable that only the more important aspects have been included. It is important to remember, when looking at the general trend, that many of the ideas were first tried out long before they attained general acceptance. Such items as revolving guns, multi-barrelled guns, repeating guns and breech-loading guns were all tried out in the era of the matchlock and flintlock. Their expense, black-powder fouling and the limitation imposed by early types of ignition were some of the major reasons for their restricted use at that time.

To sum up: guns have throughout their history consisted of a tube blocked by some means at one end, in which has been placed a propellant charge and a bullet or shot. There have been three main means of ignition: by smouldering match, by spark from pyrites or flint and steel and by percussion or detonation. The greatest advances in gun technology became possible once detonating cap, propellant and bullet or shot were combined in the centre-fire cartridge.

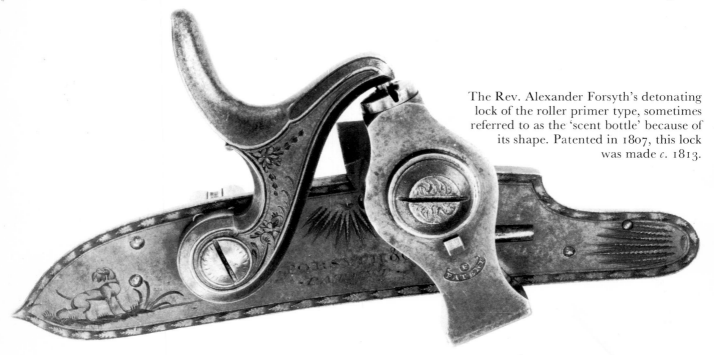

The Rev. Alexander Forsyth's detonating lock of the roller primer type, sometimes referred to as the 'scent bottle' because of its shape. Patented in 1807, this lock was made c. 1813.

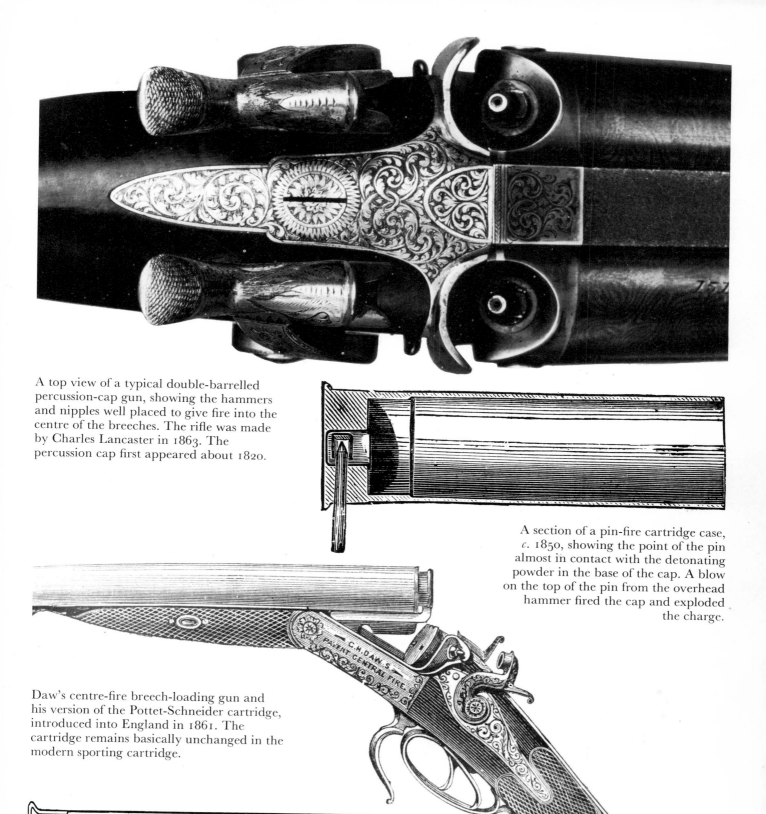

A top view of a typical double-barrelled percussion-cap gun, showing the hammers and nipples well placed to give fire into the centre of the breeches. The rifle was made by Charles Lancaster in 1863. The percussion cap first appeared about 1820.

A section of a pin-fire cartridge case, *c*. 1850, showing the point of the pin almost in contact with the detonating powder in the base of the cap. A blow on the top of the pin from the overhead hammer fired the cap and exploded the charge.

Daw's centre-fire breech-loading gun and his version of the Pottet-Schneider cartridge, introduced into England in 1861. The cartridge remains basically unchanged in the modern sporting cartridge.

The gun in warfare

Guns were probably first employed in warfare at the battle of Crécy in 1346, when some early form of cannon was used. Various crude handguns followed which at first in no way rivalled the longbow or crossbow, except in the terrifying effect of their noise and smoke on those who had not faced them before.

The knights at first had their armour strengthened in an attempt to render it bullet proof. Soon, however, as guns improved, the weight of armour necessary to stop a lead ball so encumbered the knight that he was severely handicapped. The use of guns was to effect a profound change in the balance of arms. The knight with his great skill with sword and lance, though clad in his superbly-wrought armour, could now be humbled in the dust by a foot soldier armed with a gun. The bowman too, proud of his skill derived from years of constant practice, found his place being taken by the arquebusiers whose skill with a gun was more easily acquired. Massed formations of pikemen, a speciality of the Swiss mercenaries, found themselves vulnerable to field artillery and infantry armed with matchlock guns. They were mown down in such large numbers at the battle of Bicocca in 1552 that from then on pikemen were largely confined to the rôle of supporting the ranks of arquebusiers.

By 1600 the gun was established in Europe as the successor to the bow. In England the longbow, once so successful on the battlefields of Europe, was at last officially relinquished in 1595. Musketeers supported by pikemen and field artillery formed the main body of European armies and often proved themselves more than equal to heavily-armoured cavalry.

Matchlock guns were produced in a variety of lengths and bore sizes, according to the use for which they were designed. There was some confusion amongst contemporary writers in the naming of the different classes of gun and terms varied from country to country. However, in England by about 1600 the musket emerged as the standard infantry weapon with a barrel 4 feet in length and of 10 bore. Gun bores were calculated according to the number of lead balls of the diameter of the bore that went to make one pound, so the greater the number the smaller the bore. There were intermediate guns called 'calivers' and 'arquebuses' with shorter barrels and of about sixteen bore, and there were lighter guns, mostly carried by cavalry, called 'carbines' and 'petronels' which had the shortest barrels of all, and were about twenty-four bore. Many of these carbines and the long-barrelled pistols used by cavalry were fitted with wheel-locks for the obvious reason that a matchlock was very difficult for a mounted man to manage.

Cavalry, having discarded their heavy armour, were able to give full scope to their natural mobility and dash. German cavalrymen, termed *reiter*, were armed with three wheel-lock pistols. They were noted for one particular tactic, that of charging in successive lines close up to the enemy ranks, discharging their pistols and wheeling away. These wheel-lock pistols were elegant long-barrelled pieces with clean-cut plain steel locks and mounts. The richly-decorated pistols of this type – with their chiselled and engraved locks and mounts, and stocks inlaid with stagshorn – were mostly made for noblemen who carried them on ceremonial occasions in their saddle holsters and enjoyed them as works of art.

The Thirty Years' War, which started in 1618, involved

Part of a series of engravings, *c.* 1600, showing a musketeer's drill for loading, priming and firing his musket. He uses a rest and has his charges suspended from a bandolier over his shoulder. He keeps his priming powder in a small flask suspended on his left side.

Guard, blow and open your pan.

Present.

Give Fire.

Dismount your musket.

Uncock your match.

Return your match

Clear your pan.

Prime your pan.

Shut your pan.

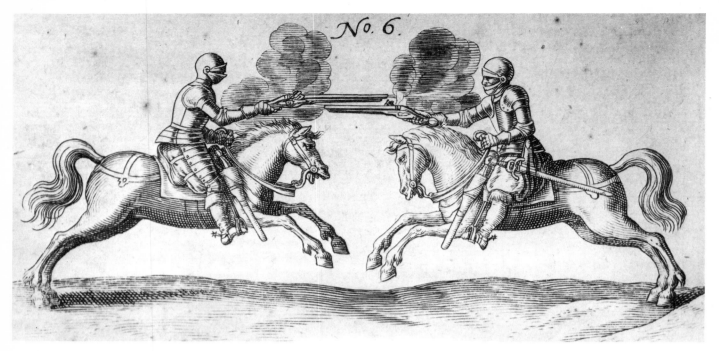

An engraving from *Art Militaire à Cheval* by Jean Jacques de Wallhausen, Frankfurt, 1616, showing the use of wheel-lock pistols by the armoured cavalry of the period

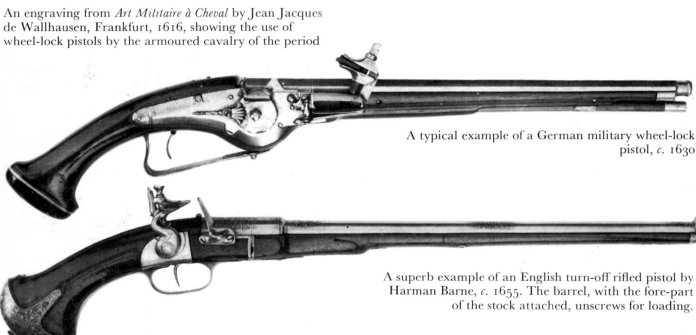

A typical example of a German military wheel-lock pistol, *c.* 1630

A superb example of an English turn-off rifled pistol by Harman Barne, *c.* 1655. The barrel, with the fore-part of the stock attached, unscrews for loading.

most of Europe. It gave rise to a military genius, Gustavus Adolphus, King of Sweden, a master of military organization, strategy and tactics who had a strong influence on the conduct of warfare in the seventeenth century.

Appreciating the use of infantry firepower, he increased the proportion of musketeers to pikemen and also improved the mobility of musketeers by making their muskets shorter and lighter so that they no longer needed a stand to fire them. He also introduced paper cartridges to speed up loading, the cartridge being torn open with the teeth, a little powder placed in the priming pan and the remainder down the barrel followed by the rest of the paper cartridge, including the ball. The paper cartridge thus acted as both patch and wad for the

ball and gave it a reasonably gas-tight fit. It was usual for musket balls to be smaller than the bore for ease of loading. Because musket barrels fouled up quite badly after a number of shots it was very difficult to ram home a tight-fitting bullet, and, as speed of loading and firing volleys was the important thing, a smaller ball was the obvious solution.

Gustavus used his musketeers and pikemen in a mutual-support system in which each unit was able to carry out its natural rôle. In defence or attack the fence of pikes gave the musketeers security from which they assailed the enemy with steady volleys. Gustavus's cavalry abandoned the ineffective manoeuvre of stopping short of the enemy to fire volleys of pistol shots. Instead they charged forward at a gallop with

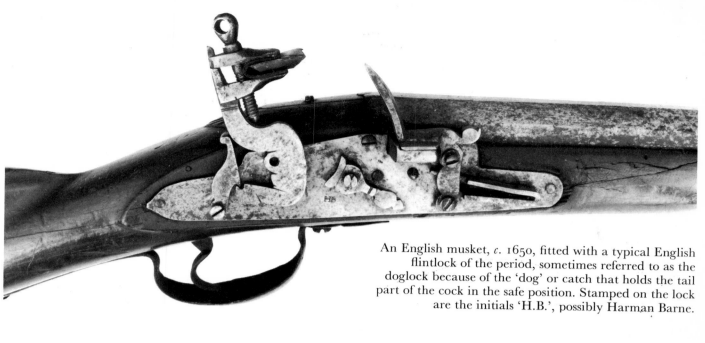

An English musket, *c.* 1650, fitted with a typical English flintlock of the period, sometimes referred to as the doglock because of the 'dog' or catch that holds the tail part of the cock in the safe position. Stamped on the lock are the initials 'H.B.', possibly Harman Barne.

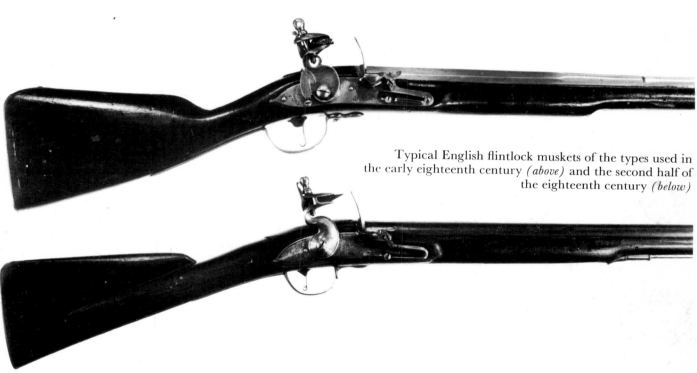

Typical English flintlock muskets of the types used in the early eighteenth century *(above)* and the second half of the eighteenth century *(below)*

sword in hand, keeping their pistols in reserve for use in the general mêlée. Thus they were able to carry the full momentum of the charge into the heart of the enemy. Gustavus used his mobile field artillery to soften up large enemy formations as a prelude to attacks by combined musketeers and pikemen, or his cavalry.

England had stood apart from the struggles in Europe but was herself embroiled in civil war in 1642. In the early days of the struggle the infantry were, for the most part, hastily-raised irregulars armed with an assortment of weapons. The muskets included matchlocks, snaphances and the early English flintlock or doglock, and a few wheel-locks. Contemporary reference was made to the use of rifles of the turn-off type by keepers of deer parks. The barrels of these rifles unscrewed at the breech, allowing the charge to be placed in the breech with the ball resting in a cavity on top; the barrel was then screwed on again. These rifles had the advantage that the ball completely filled the bore and had not been damaged by ramming it from the muzzle. Contemporary accounts suggest that these rifles were used to good effect, especially for 'picking off' the enemy at considerable distances during sieges.

At first the Royalist cavalry led by Prince Rupert of the Rhine showed its superiority over that of Parliament. Composed of well-mounted and experienced horsemen, they followed the dashing Prince Rupert sword in hand, in the

An English flintlock
cavalry pistol, *c.* 1710

manner of Gustavus, relying on the momentum of the charge and using their pistols only as secondary weapons. These pistols were mostly long-barrelled holster pistols fired by wheel-locks or the English doglock. There were, however, some pistols of the rifled turn-off type that operated on the same principle as that described for turn-off rifles. Prince Rupert, who constantly experimented with guns, used pistols of this type and proudly demonstrated their accuracy to his cousin Charles I by hitting a cock on a church steeple with successive shots. By ensuring a tight-fitting bullet it was possible to make a shorter-barrelled pistol of this type shoot with sufficient power to penetrate a breast-plate.

In the winter of 1642–3 Oliver Cromwell raised a regiment of cavalry in East Anglia. Recruited from good material, rigorously trained and well disciplined, these 'Ironsides' were welded into an efficient fighting force. They wore a helmet, back- and breast-plates over a buff coat and were armed with a sword, a pair of pistols and a carbine.

At Marston Moor in 1644 Prince Rupert's cavalry in a wild charge swept much of the Parliamentary force from the field but carried the pursuit too far, believing the battle won. Cromwell and his regiment then charged the flank of the Royalist infantry in a steady, disciplined manner and after a hard fight destroyed them.

In the reorganization of the Parliamentary forces that followed, further cavalry regiments were raised on the same lines and also a regiment of dragoons. Mounted and armed with sword and musket, dragoons were trained to skirmish mounted or fight on foot as required. Their mobility and versatility were great assets. The musketeers of the New Model Army, as it was called, wore red tunics and were armed with a lighter type of musket that needed no rest, mostly using the English flintlock or doglock. For every two musketeers there was a supporting pikeman, armed with a sword and a 16-foot pike; he wore a helmet and body armour. Parliament's New Model Army could well be described as Britain's first regular army. The red of the musketeers' coats was to remain the colour of British infantry until the end of the nineteenth century.

It was customary at this time for orders for the various muskets and pistols to be placed by the Board of Ordnance. Many were made by liverymen of the Worshipful Company of Gunmakers (founded in 1637), working in the vicinity of the Tower of London.

The War of the Spanish Succession (1701–13) was the result of France's dreams of glory and her attempts to dominate Europe. The war brought to the fore one of the greatest of military leaders, John Churchill, better known by the title he earned, that of 1st Duke of Marlborough.

Marlborough had all the qualities that go to make an ideal military commander. A great leader of men, he won their affection and confidence and was ever mindful of their welfare. He was a master of administration, strategy and tactics, and he also had the diplomatic skill to hold his allies together.

Marlborough perfected the cavalry tactics of Gustavus and Cromwell, charging at a steady pace in three ranks with sword in hand. This was sound practice, for to draw a pistol from its holster, cock, aim, fire and then replace it while managing an excited horse put severe limitations on its effectiveness. Also the sword continued to be effective, whereas pistols could

Above: A flintlock breech-loading rifle by Durs Egg, *c.* 1770, with a Ferguson-type screw-down breech in the lowered position

Below: A selection of Brown Bess flintlock muskets with their 17-inch socket bayonets, typical of those used by the British Army during the Napoleonic Wars.

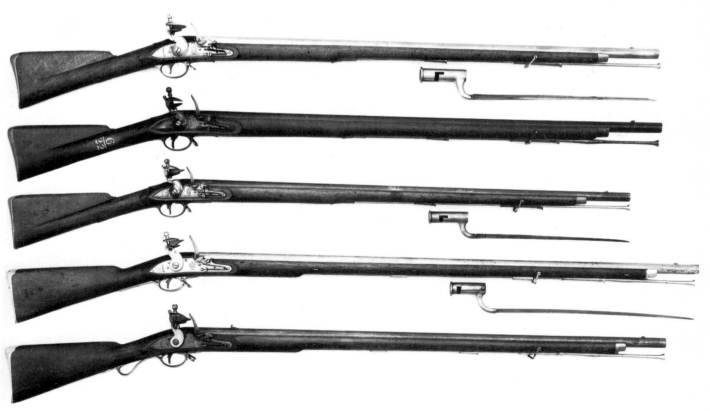

Ramillies, 1706, one of the Duke of Marlborough's great
victories. The 16th Foot fire a volley at close quarters
and charge with the bayonet. Painting by R. Simkin.

Below: The 95th, the Rifle Regiment, in action in the Pyrenees in 1813, during the latter part of the Peninsular War. Armed with the flintlock Baker rifle and clad in their dark-green uniform they were of great service to Wellington. Painting by R. Simkin.

Bottom: 'Waterloo', 1815, by Sir William Allen. The grenadiers of Napoleon's Old Guard are in disordered retreat. It is the turning point of the battle. Line defeats column as the devastating volleys of the 1st Foot Guards smash the head of the French column and the 52nd Regiment take them in the flank. The volleys are followed by a charge with the bayonet, the Old Guard retreat in disorder, and Wellington orders the general advance.

only be fired once and could not be reloaded until after the engagement had been carried through to its conclusion.

An important change in the infantry was brought about by the invention of the socket bayonet in 1678; this fitted round the muzzle of the musket, allowing the musket to be loaded and fired with the bayonet in place. It was a great advance on the plug bayonet which had been jammed into the muzzle of the musket. Armed with the musket and socket bayonet, the infantryman could fulfil the functions of both musketeer and pikeman. This increased the firepower of the infantry, since those who had been pikemen were now armed with musket and bayonet. There were no pikemen in the British Army after 1704. Also it increased the ability of the infantry to resist cavalry, in that each musketeer was equally a pikeman.

This new dual rôle lent itself to flexibility of manoeuvre. Infantrymen were trained to fire volleys in extended line, in order to bring the greatest firepower to bear. However, they had to be well trained and steady to stand extended in the face of massed advancing infantry. In the event of attack by cavalry they formed hollow squares, and in such a formation determined men could hold off every attempt to break through. Infantry carried from forty to sixty paper cartridges in their pouches, these greatly assisting the speed of loading.

The inspired use of his flexible and well-balanced fighting force enabled Marlborough to out-manoeuvre and defeat the French in his campaigns throughout central Europe, the battle of Blenheim being his greatest victory.

Weapons and tactics changed little during the remainder of the eighteenth century. However, in the American War of Independence (1775–83) the tactics and formations so effective on the battlefields of Europe were shown to be completely unsuited to conditions in America. In unfamiliar country, the British Army's red coats and tight formations made them sitting targets for camouflaged irregulars shooting from cover. The American frontiersmen had learned this style of fighting in combating Indians and were therefore experts in accurate rifle shooting from cover.

As the war went on some attempts were made to meet the new situation. Numbers of German riflemen were recruited, armed with rifles similar to the German hunting rifles. Also Captain Patrick Ferguson in command of the Light Company of the 71st Regiment had been experimenting with his famous breech-loading rifles. He had gone as far as arming his Light Company with these rifles and training the men in their use. These flintlock rifles had a vertical screw which was attached to the trigger-guard. This wound down to open the breech; the ball and powder were put in position, and the screw was wound up. It then required only a little powder to be placed in the priming pan and the rifle was loaded. As a single turn of the screw opened or closed the breech, it could be loaded and fired about four times per minute, a considerable rate for that period. There were other advantages, in that a tight-fitting ball could be used undamaged by ramming and that the rifle could be loaded while the rifleman remained lying down in low cover, unlike a muzzle-loader, which had to be loaded upright.

There were several engagements in which the riflemen used their Ferguson rifles with telling effect against American backwoodsmen, but Captain Ferguson was killed at the battle of Kings Mountain in South Carolina when the militia he commanded were surrounded and defeated by a superior force. Ferguson had received little official support for his revolutionary rifle and with his death the whole project was dropped.

Just when the affectionate name 'Brown Bess' was first used by the British soldier to describe his musket is something of a mystery. The name is now applied to the series of muskets which developed from the Long Land musket with its distinctive brass furniture that came into service around 1720. This graceful and well-made musket had a 46-inch barrel of 11 bore (.75 inch) and was at first supplied with a wooden ramrod; however, as this was liable to be broken in action it was later replaced with an iron one.

A Short Land pattern with a 42-inch barrel was also introduced for use by marines and dragoons and in 1768 this became the standard musket for all, the Long Land musket being gradually phased out. The East India Company used a cheaper and more easily-made version of the Short Land pattern with a 39-inch barrel, generally known as the India pattern. Muskets being in short supply on the outbreak of war with France, it was decided in 1794 to adopt and manufacture large numbers of the India pattern. A very fine musket known as the Duke of Richmond's pattern designed in 1790 by the famous Henry Nock had to be abandoned because of the urgent need for quantity rather than quality. However, a well-made pattern of the Brown Bess, the last to be designed, was introduced gradually from about 1802. All the Brown Besses carried the 17-inch socket bayonet.

It was customary for the Board of Ordnance to order the various parts of the muskets in bulk, mostly in the London or Birmingham areas, and to store them in the Tower. The setting-up of the muskets was undertaken by London gunmakers specializing in the work, many of whom had their workshops in the Minories close by the Tower.

Although Captain Ferguson's breech-loading rifle had been abandoned, the military authorities had at last realized the desirability of having some men skilled in the use of a rifle. After a series of trials at Woolwich in 1800, the rifle designed by Ezekiel Baker was chosen as most suitable for British military requirements. This had a 30-inch barrel which was rifled with seven grooves, having a quarter turn within the barrel length. It fired patched balls of twenty to the pound. The general design of this rifle was based on the German hunting rifle; it weighed $9\frac{1}{2}$ pounds, had a brass patchbox in the side of the butt, and was fitted with a sword bayonet with a 23-inch blade.

The French Revolutionary wars, the subsequent rise of Napoleon Bonaparte and his insatiable appetite for glory and plunder kept all Europe in a state of war from 1792 to 1815. Having subjugated most of Europe, Napoleon found himself opposed by Britain and two of her most famous commanders: on sea Horatio Nelson and on land the Duke of Wellington. Nelson's great victories – the Nile 1798, Copenhagen 1801, and Trafalgar 1805 – are well known. What may not be so well known is that he had the foresight to appreciate the usefulness of riflemen in his attack on the Danish forts at Copenhagen. Nelson had, before starting out, taken aboard a company of the newly-formed Rifle Corps, later the 95th or Rifle Regiment, armed with the Baker rifle. Their contribution to the success of the action was officially recognized in the granting

Four examples of the
British military Baker
rifle shown with its
long sword-bayonet.
Left are two rifled
carbines with swivel
ramrods. All date
from the period
1800–15.

A fine example of an officer's double-barrelled over-and-under
pistol by Staudenmayer, London, *c.* 1815. It had a swivel
ramrod and a shoulder stock, here detached, which
converted the pistol into an effective short-range carbine.

of their first battle honour, which was named 'Copenhagen'.

The riflemen of the 95th Regiment were also to earn great fame in the Peninsular campaigns, from their rearguard actions in the retreat to Corunna under Sir John Moore (1809) to the part they played in the Light Division from 1810 to 1814, when under the command of Wellington. They fought in all the major battles of the Peninsular campaign, including the final one, in France at Toulouse.

The following account illustrates the effectiveness of rifle fire at the seige of Badajoz in 1812:

'I was with a party of men behind the advanced sap, and had the opportunity of doing some mischief. Three or four heavy cannon that the enemy were working were doing frightful execution amongst our artillerymen in their advanced batteries. I selected several good shots, and fired into the embrasures. In half an hour I found the guns did not go off so frequently as before I commenced this practice, and soon after gabions were stuffed into each embrasure, to stop our rifle balls from entering. They then withdrew them to fire, which was my signal for firing steadily at the embrasures. The gabions were replaced without firing the shot. I was so delighted with the good practice I was making against Johnny that I kept it up from daylight to dark, with forty as prime fellows as ever pulled trigger. These guns were literally silenced.'

Napoleon's army put great reliance on artillery and tended to use infantry in massed columns. Wellington, whose forces were usually outnumbered, fully exploited the firepower of his infantry, who were trained to fire quick and steady volleys in extended line. In the Peninsula, Wellington always endeavoured to draw up his infantry out of sight over the brow of a rise or hill where they were not exposed to artillery fire. Skirmishers and riflemen were sent forward to harass the French, and horse artillery and cavalry protected the flanks. The French would advance in great columns with some line formations between them and skirmishers in front; it seemed, as they came over the brow of a hill, that the thin red line of British infantry in front of them must be swept away. On would come the French, firing at the still ranks with ordered arms ahead of them. Then, when in certain musket range, came the order to present and fire. Volley after volley from the Brown Bess muskets decimated the close-packed columns before them, throwing the ranks into confusion. And, as the French recoiled, the British with a great shout would advance to complete the rout with the bayonet.

Napoleon and Wellington were to meet in battle for the first time at Waterloo. Napoleon had not changed his tactics, believing that defeats in the Peninsula were due to the fact that the generals concerned lacked his ability. He therefore attacked in his old style with massive infantry formations after artillery bombardment. This attack was contained by the fire of allied infantry and field artillery and then utterly routed by the magnificent charge of the heavy cavalry. The next major phase of the battle involved alternate pounding by artillery and massive attacks by cavalry, forcing the allied infantry to take refuge in their square formations. In these squares they were able to resist the cavalry attacks but suffered sadly from artillery fire in between attacks.

Above: 'The battle of Waterloo' by Felix Philippoteaux, cuirassiers charging a square of Highlanders. In a series of tremendous charges French cavalry regiments led by Marshal Ney carried out massed attacks on the British squares, which, though battered, remained unbroken. Steady discipline, close-range musket volleys and the tight hedge of bayonets defeated the most valiant efforts of some of the finest cavalry of the day.

Right: The battle of Balaclava, Crimean War, 1854. The 93rd, the Sutherland Highlanders, form the famous 'thin red line' that stood between the Allied supply base of Balaclava and a determined charge by a far superior force of Russian cavalry. Steady accurate rifle fire checked and repulsed the cavalry. Painting by R. Simkin.

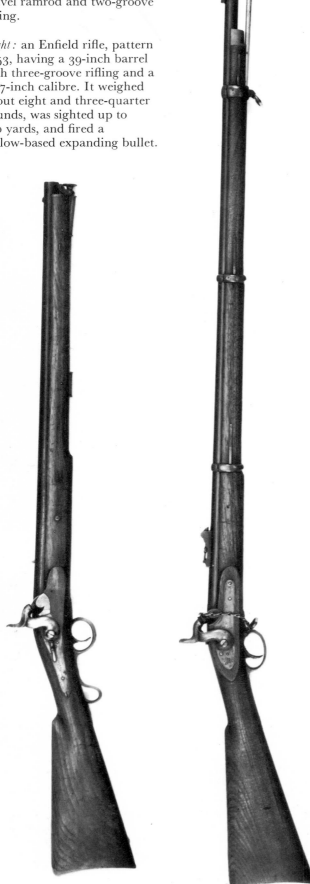

Below: a Brunswick carbine, *c.* 1840, with a back-action lock, a swivel ramrod and two-groove rifling.

Right: an Enfield rifle, pattern 1853, having a 39-inch barrel with three-groove rifling and a .577-inch calibre. It weighed about eight and three-quarter pounds, was sighted up to 900 yards, and fired a hollow-based expanding bullet.

Believing the decimated ranks in front of him to be capable of little further resistance, Napoleon unleashed his finest troops, the famous grenadiers of the Old Guard. The grenadiers came on steadily, ignoring the fire of field artillery; as they came over the brow of the hill and saw no opposition they thought that victory and the road to Brussels lay before them. However, the 1st Foot Guards were lying under cover of the bank of a sunken road, safe from artillery fire. Wellington called to their commander, 'Now Maitland, now's your time.' At a word of command the Foot Guards leapt up as if on parade, presented and fired devastating close-range volleys, mowing down the front ranks of the Old Guard and throwing the others into confusion. Colborne, seeing his opportunity, attacked the Old Guard in the flank with the 52nd Regiment and two battalions of the 95th. Then the Foot Guards charged with the bayonet and the Old Guard recoiled in disorder down the slope. It was the turning point of the battle. Seeing the French demoralized by the defeat of their 'invincible' Guard, Wellington, by a forward wave of his hat, signalled the general advance. With the Prussians attacking all along their right flank, Napoleon and his army fled the field. Once again musket volleys in line had proved their effectiveness against massed columns.

In the peace that followed it was not until the late 1830s that the percussion cap at last replaced the flintlock on muskets. It was also used on the Brunswick rifle, which replaced the Baker in 1838. The new rifle had a 30-inch barrel with a .704-inch calibre and deep two-groove rifling designed to fire a belted ball, that is a ball with a raised band round it that fitted into the grooves.

William Greener, an English gunmaker, had tried unsuccessfully to interest the Board of Ordnance in the principle of an expanding, elongated bullet for a muzzle-loading rifle. The point being that it was easy to load, but on being fired a wedge was forced into the hollow cup of its base, making it key strongly into the rifling and give a good gas-tight fit. However, when a French officer, Captain Minié, designed a similar device with an iron cup that was forced up into the base. The Minié rifled musket was replaced in 1853 by the Board showed interest. The result was the Minié rifled musket of 1851, which had a 39-inch barrel of .577-inch calibre, rifled with three wide shallow grooves. The bullet was a modified version of the Minié, having a boxwood plug in the base. The Minié rifled-musket was replaced in 1853 by the well-designed Enfield rifle. These rifles did good service in the Crimea and also in the Indian Mutiny.

In the Crimean War (1854-6), during which Britain, France, Turkey and Sardinia were allied against Russia, tactics were much the same as they had been at Waterloo. Heroism and discipline lower down the scale to some extent compensated for the inept leadership of the higher command. At the battle of the Alma the Guards and the Highlanders advanced in perfectly-dressed ranks up the hill to capture the strongly-held great battery and were then mistakenly ordered to retire; the hill was promptly recovered by the Russians. Against even stiffer opposition, the steady ranks again had to storm and take the hill. At Balaclava the Light Brigade charged the guns in the old style with sword and lance, and the Heavy Brigade successfully charged a far larger force of Russian cavalry, sword in hand, in much the same style in which they charged at Waterloo, almost forty years before.

The use of rifled muskets had not as yet had much effect on tactics and formations but one action at Balaclava was to show what could be done. The famous 'thin red line', consisting of a battalion of the 93rd or Sutherland Highlanders drawn up in two ranks, stood between Balaclava harbour and a large force of Russian cavalry that seemed unstoppable. By steady fire they halted and repulsed the cavalry.

Returning to look at the development of the military pistol, officers had generally purchased their pistols privately, often from some of the best gunmakers of the time. In the eighteenth century these were mostly of the full-stocked holster-pistol type, sometimes fitted with belt hooks when used by infantry or naval officers.

During the Napoleonic Wars a variety of pistols, often of very fine quality, were used by officers. Amongst them were single-barrelled pistols of various bores, including full musket-bore, fitted with swivel ramrods that could not be lost. There were also double-barrelled pistols designed on the side-by-side or under-and-over principle. A favourite of some officers was a single-barrelled or double-barrelled over-and-under pistol, fitted with a detachable shoulder stock. With the addition of this stock the pistol became a very useful short carbine, especially when it was rifled. Many officers setting out for the Crimea placed their faith in one of the new percussion revolving pistols. These pistols were of three main types: the 'pepperbox', having an average of five barrels, revolvers such as the Adams that cocked and fired when the trigger was

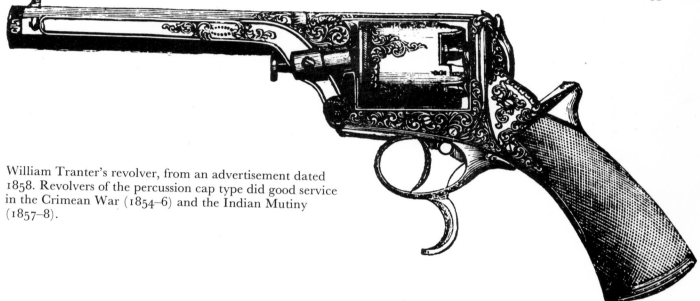

William Tranter's revolver, from an advertisement dated 1858. Revolvers of the percussion cap type did good service in the Crimean War (1854–6) and the Indian Mutiny (1857–8).

The Snider breech, designed in 1864, by which British muzzle-loading rifles were converted to breech-loading. The breech is shown in the open position.

A section of .577 Boxer centre-fire cartridge designed for the Snider rifle. Patented by Colonel Boxer in 1866, it had a grease-grooved bullet with a hollow base and a boxwood wedge-plug.

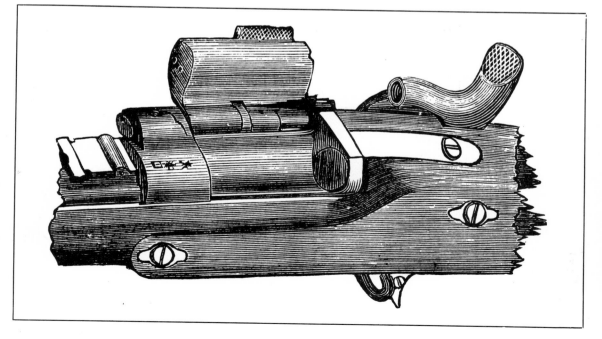

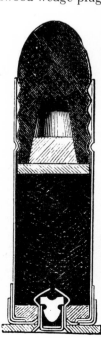

Below: The battle of the Alma, Crimean War, 1854: 'Forward 42nd', a painting by Robert Gibb. The long lines of Highlanders and Guards move up the hill in well-ordered ranks to storm and capture the Russian batteries. Moving forward in the old style in closely-formed ranks was to become too costly an operation due to the increased efficiency of rifle fire. This was one of the last occasions on which such formations were successful.

pulled, and the Colt revolver that had to be cocked with the thumb before it could be fired.

Samuel Colt had strenuously publicized his revolvers in England, beginning by exhibiting them at the Great Exhibition of 1851. He managed to gain a contract to supply large numbers of the Navy pattern to the Board of Admiralty, who had heard that the Russians were equipping their Navy with revolvers. The Admiralty were obviously still thinking in terms of boarding parties.

Revolving pistols must have been particularly useful in the battle of Inkerman where the fighting was confused and at close quarters. The Board of Ordnance were sufficiently impressed with the Adams revolver to adopt the double-action officially in 1856. This revolver could be cocked by the thumb and fired with deliberate aim or, for quick shooting, by just pulling the trigger. It was later converted to use metallic centre-fire cartridges.

The American Civil War (1861–5) saw a change in tactics brought about by improved percussion muskets, rifles and carbines. A variety of weapons was used by both sides, notably from the Springfield, Sharps and Colt factories. The defensive power of rifle fire was demonstrated in actions where infantry fired from the protection of shallow trenches or breastworks. The solid formations of cavalry and infantry familiar on European battlefields would have proved disastrous.

Samuel Colt's mass-production methods held a portent of the future harnessing of industrial power to warfare. The invention of the first practical machine gun by Richard Gatling in 1862 was the earliest indication of the way in which the machine gun's firepower was to revolutionize the warfare of the future. Only small numbers of his crank-operated, six-barrelled early model were used in the Civil War, but in 1866 he was given an order by the United States Army for one hundred guns and by this time he had developed a model capable of firing at the rate of 1,200 rounds per minute.

In Europe the lessons to be learned from the American conflict were largely ignored. However, there was soon to be a rude awakening nearer home. Prussia under Bismarck was being systematically organized for war. In 1848 the Prussian military authorities adopted the needle-fire breech-loading rifle invented by Von Dreyse. This was the first military rifle to have the breech closed by the now-familiar bolt action. The non-metallic cartridge had the fulminate in the base of the bullet, and this was fired by a needle-like firing pin that passed through the powder charge to strike the fulminate. There were two main drawbacks to the rifle: the needle was at the centre of the explosion and therefore liable to soften and break, and the closure of the breech was not entirely gas tight, giving an unpleasant flash-back.

In spite of these failings the Dreyse rifle was remarkably more effective than existing muzzle-loaders. There was consternation in European military circles after its success in Prussia's short war with Denmark in 1864 and the Seven Weeks' War with Austria in 1866. These spectacular victories alarmed the major European powers into an urgent attempt to equip their armies with comparable rifles.

The French adopted in 1866 the rifle invented by Antoine Chassepot. This was also a bolt-action needle-fire rifle but it had the advantage that the needle struck the percussion cap in the rear end of the combustible cartridge and therefore did not suffer from being in the centre of the explosion as in the Dreyse. The Chassepot also had longer range, better accuracy and was better sealed at the breech. It did, however, tend to foul up in the breech, making it difficult to load the soft cartridge, and the smaller-calibre barrel also fouled badly after a number of shots.

The Franco-Prussian War provided a foretaste of the organization of a nation's resources for war in Prussia's carefully planned mobilization and transportation of troops in a pre-arranged plan of campaign. The training, staff work and planning were inspired and dovetailed by Von Moltke, the chief of the Prussian general staff, who might be described as the architect of modern warfare.

French leadership at the top was sadly lacking but her soldiers fought well and there were heavy casualties on both sides. However better organization and leadership gave victory to the Prussians. The defensive firepower of breech-loading rifles, for all their limitations, was clearly demonstrated in the conflict.

At Saint-Privat the advance of the Prussian Guard was halted by a line of French armed with Chassepots, the Prussians suffering 8,000 casualties in twenty minutes. French cavalry charging in the old style at Worth was quickly broken up by rifle fire. The Prussians, having surrounded a large part of the French Army at Sedan, profited by their previous experience and smashed the French infantry with artillery fire from beyond the range of their Chassepot rifles.

The British Army also appreciated the need for a breech-loading rifle, and various ideas were tried out. Calisher and Terry's capping breech-loader was given an extensive trial aboard HMS Excellent in 1858 and issued experimentally to some cavalry units. Westley Richards also produced a capping breech-loading carbine in 1858, often called the 'monkey tail' because of the top lever which lifted up and forwards to open the breech. This carbine was approved for issue to cavalry in 1861 and was subsequently issued to yeomanry regiments. These capping breech-loaders used a paper cartridge but were fired by a separate percussion cap placed on the exterior nipple.

The need for a breech-loading rifle for general use led to the adoption in 1865 of Jacob Snider's system for the conversion of the Enfield rifle to take a centre-fire paper-cased cartridge with a metal base. The breech-block that hinged on the right-hand side contained an angled striking-pin that was struck by the hammer. The first coiled-paper centre-fire cartridge with a papier-mâché base was improved and strengthened by Colonel Boxer in 1867 when he substituted

Above right: The American Civil War, 1861-5. Riflemen firing from behind defences such as this inflicted very heavy casualties on massed attacks of infantry or cavalry. A Brady photograph of the stone wall and sunken road at Fredericksburg showing Confederate dead.

Right: An incident in the Franco-Prussian War, 1870-1. The French defence of the cemetary of Saint-Privat in which the Prussians suffered heavy casualties in the face of concentrated fire from Chassepot rifles.

Isandhlwana, 1879. A British force of some six thousand men was almost wiped out in a surprise attack by a very large force of Zulus. The British were overwhelmed before they could use their firepower effectively. A year later at Ulundi, concentrated rifle fire defeated the Zulus.

Abu-Klea, 1885. A British column of about eleven hundred men on the way to relieve General Gordon in Khartoum was attacked by ten thousand fanatical dervishes. Because they were armed with single-shot Martini-Henry rifles, the rate of fire was insufficient to prevent the dervishes breaking into the British square. Only after the most desperate fighting did the British win the day.

Breech-loading needle-fire rifles: *(above)* the Prussian version, invented by Von Dreyse and adopted by the Prussian Army in 1848, and *(below)* the French version, invented by Antoine Chassepot and adopted by the French Army in 1866

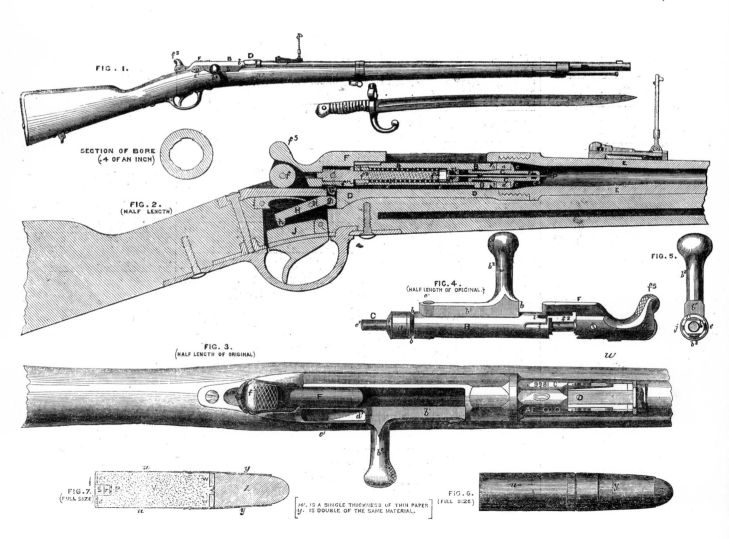

FIG. 1.

SECTION OF BORE
(·4 OF AN INCH)

FIG. 2.
(HALF LENGTH)

FIG. 4.
(HALF LENGTH OF ORIGINAL)

FIG. 5.

FIG. 3.
(HALF LENGTH OF ORIGINAL)

FIG. 7.
(FULL SIZE)

[W. IS A SINGLE THICKNESS OF THIN PAPER
y. IS DOUBLE OF THE SAME MATERIAL.]

FIG. 6.
(FULL SIZE)

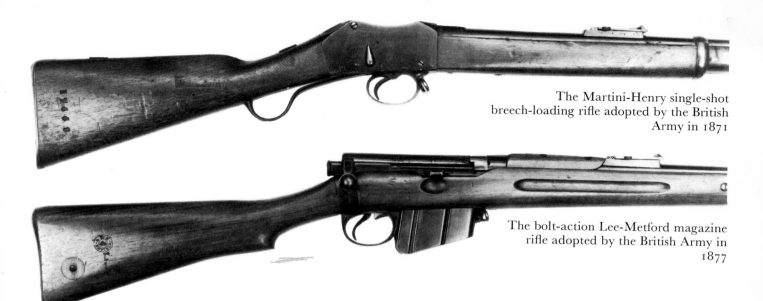

The Martini-Henry single-shot
breech-loading rifle adopted by the British
Army in 1871

The bolt-action Lee-Metford magazine
rifle adopted by the British Army in
1877

an iron-disc base and a thin brass case that expanded to give a gas-tight fit.

The makeshift Snider was followed by the Martini-Henry rifle in 1871. This single-shot breech-loader used the Martini falling-block action operated by a lever behind the trigger-guard. It had a 33-inch barrel of .450-inch calibre with rifling designed by Alexander Henry, the Edinburgh gunmaker. In the first instance the Boxer cartridge was adapted for use with the Martini-Henry. During the Egyptian campaign this was found liable to jam and was replaced with a solid-drawn brass case in 1885. The standard rifle was just over four feet long, weighed $8\frac{1}{2}$ pounds and was sighted up to 1,450 yards. Carbines were also made with 22-inch barrels, the calibre of some of the later ones being reduced to .400.

Improvements in all arms were particularly rapid in the last quarter of the nineteenth century and military arms were no exception. No sooner had single-shot rifles been perfected, using the brass-cased centre-fire cartridge, than all the major powers set about finding some sort of bolt-action magazine rifle designed to fire a smaller-calibre jacketed bullet. The tendency had been for the bores of military rifles to be smaller and for bullets to become more elongated; by the 1890s .300 was the average.

Britain had first adopted the Lee magazine-system bolt-action rifle in 1877; as the rifle also used the shallow-groove rifling designed by Metford, it was given the name 'Lee-Metford'. The improved Mark II version of 1893 had a barrel 30 inches long of .303 calibre, sighted up to 2,900 yards. The nickel-cased lead bullet was propelled by a cordite charge, for by the 1890s the major powers had turned to one or other of the smokeless nitro powders. These smokeless powders were a great advantage from a military point of view because the smoke of black powder had always given away the position and numbers of riflemen. Smokeless powder was also cleaner and did not foul up the barrel and breeches. The magazine of the Lee-Metford Mark II held ten cartridges in two columns, and loading was made easy by means of the cartridge clip, holding five cartridges, that had been invented by Mannlicher in 1885.

A great advantage of the high-velocity rifles adopted by most nations in the 1890s was the flatter trajectory. Judging distance exactly was not so critical as in the previous lower-velocity weapons where the drop of the bullet was considerable, especially after the first 150 yards. In the second half of the nineteenth century Britain was involved in numerous colonial wars and punitive expeditions. In spite of the fact that the British forces were often unsuitably equipped for the climate and country and slow to adapt their tactics, firepower, steady discipline and courage usually won in the end. But due to indecisiveness a British force which had left a defensive position was surrounded and annihilated at Maiwand in India in 1880. And in the Zulu War in 1879 a British force was overwhelmed by the speed and manoeuvrability of superior numbers of Zulus. The well-organized and disciplined battle formation of the Zulus may be likened to the horns of a buffalo, massive in the centre, with horns at either side to envelop the enemy. However, later in the year at Ulundi, the Zulu Army was shattered and defeated by steady concentrated rifle fire.

The Boer War of 1899–1902 forcibly impressed upon the British Army the effectiveness of accurate rifle fire by an enemy who not only had excellent marksmen but made full use of their knowledge of the country. The Boers were mostly armed with the Mauser magazine rifle, but some used various sporting rifles with which they were used to shooting game at long distances on the open veld.

Weapons of various types had advanced rapidly in the last quarter of the nineteenth century, an advance that was facilitated by the use of metallic cartridges. In 1887 the British Army and Navy adopted the famous Webley .45-inch revolver, which automatically ejected the spent cartridges on being opened for reloading. This was to be manufactured in very large numbers in the First and Second World Wars.

A number of semi-automatic or self-loading pistols were produced (usually referred to as automatic pistols). One of the first automatic pistols to be successful was that designed by Hugo Borchardt in 1893; this used a box magazine inserted in the grip. In 1898 George Luger developed this principle into the well-known Luger pistol. The Mauser 10-shot automatic pistol, also of 1898, was reliable and popular. Winston

Churchill used one of these pistols when charging with the 21st Lancers at Omdurman in 1898. He fired all ten rounds from his pistol before emerging from the thick of the dervishes and probably owed his life to the fact that he had decided to use a pistol rather than a sword because of an injury to his shoulder received while playing polo. Colt manufactured a model designed by John Browning which was adopted in .45-inch calibre for the United States Army in 1911; the Royal Navy adopted the .455-inch Webley in 1912, and numerous other variations of the original designs followed.

Used in both World Wars was the famous short Lee-Enfield rifle, perhaps the best made and most accurate rifle with which the British Army has been issued. It was the rapid and accurate rifle fire by superbly-trained regular soldiers that held the line in the early stages of the First World War. Such was the rapidity and accuracy of the fire on some occasions that it was mistaken for machine-gun fire by the Germans. Concentrated accurate rifle fire that would have been ideal in the conditions prevailing in South Africa was soon to be to some extent superseded by the increasing use of machine guns.

The metallic centre-fire cartridge was also to make the machine gun a practical proposition. The first successful machine gun was patented by Hiram Maxim in 1884. This recoil-operated machine gun was belt fed and water cooled; it was adopted in 1889 by the British Army in .450-inch calibre but subsequent models were changed to .303-inch. The later British Vickers Mark I was a modification of the Maxim. Many of the nations of the world adopted the Maxim, including the Germans who used it in the First World War.

The gas-operated Hotchkiss machine gun of 1895 had an air-cooled barrel and was fed with strips of cartridges. The 1914 heavy model was used by the French in the First World War. John Browning also designed a gas-operated machine gun, which he had perfected by 1895. His 1901 recoil-operated model was later modified into the United States M1917 water-cooled and M1919 air-cooled machine guns and numerous other versions. There were also lighter machine guns, one of the first being the Madsen recoil-operated magazine-fed gun of 1903. There followed the well-known Lewis gun of the First World War, which was gas operated and fed by a drum-type magazine. The French used the recoil-operated M1915 Chauchat.

The machine gun revolutionized tactics in the First World War. It was largely responsible for the stalemate of trench warfare: a situation in which large-scale infantry attacks, even after artillery preparation, could be cut to pieces by machine-gun fire inflicting devastating losses.

In two spheres, future events were anticipated. Whereas the cavalry still dreamed of charges with sword and lance, more practical men designed the 'tank'. This armoured monster for all its early imperfections was at last an answer to barbed wire and the machine gun. The cavalry reconnaissance rôle was also largely taken over, by the Flying Corps, who in their flimsy aircraft found new freedom of movement in the air. As skirmishes between aircraft increased, the makeshift weapons carried by them gave way to properly-fitted machine guns, timed with the engine to shoot between the blades of the propeller.

The Second World War showed the power and rapid manoeuvrability of tanks supported by aircraft; it also demonstrated the value of shock troops, ground or airborne, armed with light machine guns and submachine guns. Surprise, speed and firepower took precedence over static defence, which was either outflanked or smashed by new offensive techniques. The tremendous firepower of the eight converging machine guns in the wings of the Spitfire was to blunt the German offensive against Britain in the summer of 1940. The Thompson submachine gun was among the weapons supplied to Britain after Dunkirk; it was later replaced by a cheap mass-produced and somewhat erratic weapon called the 'Sten'.

Since 1945 the tendency has been for most nations to adopt gas-operated selective-automatic or semi-automatic rifles. The British, having developed the very fine .280 EM2, felt obliged to adopt the Fabrique-Nationale (FN) light automatic rifle because it fired the standard 7.62-millimetre NATO cartridge.

The fifty years from 1850 to 1900 saw the extraordinary advance from the muzzle-loader to the machine gun; it was the most intensive period of development in the entire history of the gun as we know it. Little of major significance has been added since and it would seem that the ultimate has almost been reached. It remains to be seen whether in the future a completely new concept will take its place.

Above right: The Maxim machine gun shown in action with the 62nd, The Wiltshire Regiment, near Norvals Pont during the Boer War

Right: The Boer War, 1899-1902. Mass attacks by infantry against strongly-held Boer positions and accurate rifle fire could only be pressed home with frightful casualties. So it was at the battle of Caesar's Camp, where the Devons charged on Wagon Hill at the siege of Ladysmith.

The Mauser 7.63-mm semi-automatic pistol (introduced in 1896) shown with the wooden holster which could be attached as a shoulder stock. The magazine holds ten rounds.

A British Vickers machine gun in action in the First World War, 1914-18

A British Lewis gun in action in a front-line trench near Ovillors during the battle of the Somme, July 1916

A soldier of the Netherlands Brigade manning a Bren gun during the Second World War. The Bren was a Czech-designed magazine-fed light machine gun with a quick-change barrel. Adopted by the British Army in 1935, it is still in service.

Four versions of the cheap and handy 9-mm Sten submachine gun which was manufactured in large numbers in the Second World War for British and Allied forces

The LIAI self-loading rifle firing the NATO 7·62-mm ammunition. It weighs 9½ pounds. The magazine, which holds twenty rounds, and the bayonet are shown separately.

Sporting guns and rifles

Once the matchlock had been contrived, it was not long before guns began to be used in preference to the longbow or cross-bow for shooting birds and beasts. The nobility soon commissioned fine-quality matchlock guns, and later wheel-lock rifles, to be used for shooting deer, boar and other animals found in the forests of Europe. Allied to the use of guns and rifles for hunting was the sport of target shooting and, in particular, shooting at a poppinjay. A stuffed bird or 'poppin-jay' at the top of a tall pole had already been used as a target in archery competitions long before it was used for target shooting with guns. It was useful practice for shooting such birds as pheasants and capercaille perched in the upper branches of trees after they had been flushed up by dogs.

A special type of light wheel-lock birding rifle called a *tschinke* was developed in the seventeenth century for this type of shooting. The name derives from Teschen, the old name for the Polish town of Cieszyn, where the rifle originated. The lock is interesting for the use of an external mainspring connected by a chain to the wheel. Guns of this type were often elaborately decorated with plain and stained ivory inlay and overlaid pieces of elaborately-engraved gilded metal. Like the early wheel-lock guns and rifles they were held against the cheek when fired, the weight of the barrel absorbing most of the recoil.

It was customary in the sixteenth century to net with the aid of dogs birds like partridges that were required for the table. Birding for sport was carried on with hawks, the size of the hawk being strictly regulated according to the rank of the hawker.

The peasantry soon discovered in such crude matchlock guns as they were able to afford an easier means of shooting wildfowl than that afforded by the longbow or crossbow. The gun could be loaded with a quantity of small lead pellets, giving sufficient spread at thirty yards or so to require only approximate accuracy for such targets as ducks on a pond. This type of shooting was largely a matter of augmenting the winter supply of food. There was no question of shooting at flying birds or giving a sporting chance with a matchlock gun; it was a matter of making sure of bagging as many as possible with one shot when the birds had been stalked or enticed within certain range.

In sixteenth-century England considerable annoyance was caused to the authorities because men who were duty bound

Above right : 'Pigeon Shooting, The Members of the Red House Club, 1828', an aquatint by A. G. Reeve. Mr Osbaldeston, the famous sporting squire, is shooting at the pigeon that has just been released by the trapper. Other members are betting on the result of the match.

Right : An early seventeenth-century fowler stalking partridges with his wheel-lock gun and dog. A detail from 'The Chateau de Steen' by Paul Rubens.

Below : A German flintlock *Jäger* or hunting gun by Walther a Wasungen, *c.* 1750. The chiselled decoration on the barrel and locks has a matted gold ground. The furniture and inlay on the stock are of bronze gilt.

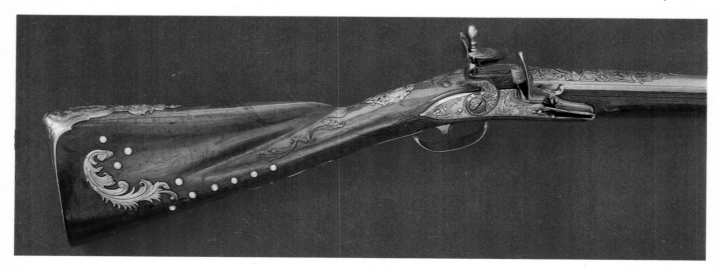

to practise with the longbow on a Sunday were instead creeping around the countryside trying to bag something for the pot with a matchlock gun. Henry VIII, being concerned with the need for archers for the defence of the realm, was obliged to legislate against such practice, but with little effect.

The art of shooting birds flying seems to have developed as a fashionable sport in France in the first half of the seventeenth century. The introduction of the French flintlock and the use of a shoulder butt made the taking of shots at flying birds practicable. There was of course a delay between pulling the trigger, the flash of the priming and the firing of the main charge; for this reason it was difficult to shoot any but birds flying almost directly away. A crossing bird would need a most delicate judgement of forward allowance, depending on both the speed of the bird and the delay in ignition.

This new idea of shooting birds flying as a fashionable sport was brought to England by Charles II and his courtiers when they returned in 1660 from their exile in France. They naturally brought with them the French fowling pieces they had been accustomed to use, and for some time sporting guns were imported from France or Italy. However, it was not long before English makers became capable of producing fine-quality sporting guns and in consequence the import of such guns lessened. Another factor that tended to restrict the use of some rather flashy but unsafe foreign guns was the tightening-up of regulations under which it was necessary that all imported guns be submitted for proof at the proof house of the Worshipful Company of Gunmakers.

Apart from the lighter type of sporting gun with its French-type lock and a barrel of about four feet, there were also long-barrelled guns – 5 to 6 feet long, with the English doglock – that were used by wildfowlers. By 1700 most guns were fitted with the French type of lock.

Richard Blome's edition of *The Gentleman's Recreation* (1686) contains a chapter on shooting which is enlivened by some most attractive engravings. These show the shooting of flying partridge from horseback, attended by servants to reload the guns and dogs to flush and retrieve the birds. Other engravings depict the use of a stalking horse for shooting duck and

the use of dogs to perch a pheasant, that is to flush it up into a tree enabling a sportsman to creep up close enough to shoot it. Shooters with very long guns are also shown firing at duck that are flying directly away from them.

The typical sporting gun of about 1700 was of the single-barrel type with a barrel averaging about forty-five inches and full stocked, that is with the wood reaching the full length of the barrel. Attractively-grained maple was popular for stocking at this time, but walnut and some fruit woods were also used. The stock was sometimes carved around the barrel tang; the side and lock plates were usually engraved with a delicate design of tendrils or slender dragons, and the escutcheon plate was large and elaborate in design. The general style of the sporting gun changed little in the first three quarters of the eighteenth century, though there was a tendency to lighter and shorter guns. The underside of the butt, which had been curved in the seventeenth century, was straightened from the grip to the toe and the butt was as a whole made narrower. Walnut became the wood generally used for stocking. Silver was used for the furniture of the better guns and brass for the others. The furniture, which included the trigger-guard, side plate, heel plate and escutcheon plate, was generally cast and chased in a variety of designs including classical, floral and sporting motifs. This period was also notable for the delicate traceries and designs carried out with silver wire inlaid into areas of the stock, particularly the butt.

In the first half of the eighteenth century Spanish barrels gained a reputation throughout Europe for their strength and shooting qualities. For this reason they were much sought after, and either the style was copied or the stamps of famous Spanish makers were deliberately forged. Their barrels are usually octagonal for the first part, with the maker's mark in gold on the top of the breech, and the longer, remaining section of the barrel up to the muzzle is round.

English eighteenth-century guns were often fitted with Spanish or Spanish-style barrels. True Spanish barrels owe their strength to the high quality of the iron used and to the forging method which ensured that the grain of the metal went round rather than along the barrel. The quality was

A superb French flintlock fowling piece, unsigned, *c.* 1675. There is fine chiselled decoration on the lock and barrel, and the stock is carved and also inlaid with silver wire.

Right: Shooting flying partridges from horseback with servants to load the guns and carry the game. An engraving from Richard Blome's edition of *The Gentleman's Recreation*, 1686.

SHOOTING FLYING

S Gribelin Sculps.

To the Honourable Thomas ⸻ Fairfax Esq.ʳˢ eldest Son of y͇
Rᵗ Honᵇˡ Henry Lord Fairfax of Denton in York=shire.⸻
This Plate is humbly Dedicated by Richard Blome.

Woodcock-shooting with a double-barrelled percussion gun. The spaniels flush the woodcock while the sportsman's groom holds his horse. Note the characteristic manner of holding a gun at this period – with the left hand well back against the trigger-guard. Painting by William Jones, *c.* 1830.

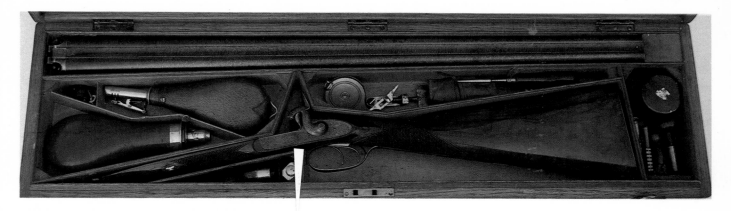

A double-barrelled 14-bore percussion gun by Charles Lancaster, London, one of the best gunmakers of his time. Made in 1857, the gun is shown in its leather-lined case with all its loading and cleaning equipment.

A fine-quality 16-bore two-groove percussion rifle made in 1853 for the Maharajah of Jodhpur, by Charles Lancaster

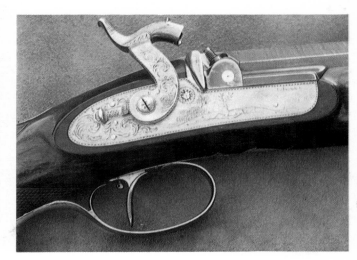

A sportsman, with dogs, shooting
ducks with his flintlock gun. An
engraving from *Abbildungen der Jagbaren
Thiere* by Ridinger, Augsburg, 1740.

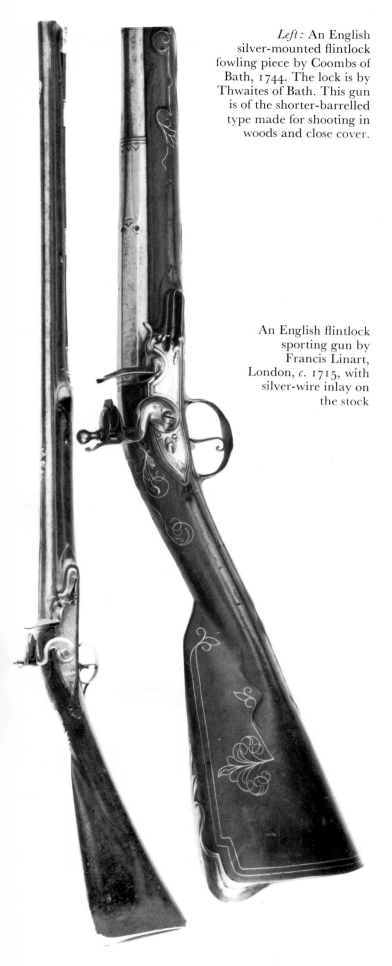

Left : An English silver-mounted flintlock fowling piece by Coombs of Bath, 1744. The lock is by Thwaites of Bath. This gun is of the shorter-barrelled type made for shooting in woods and close cover.

An English flintlock sporting gun by Francis Linart, London, *c.* 1715, with silver-wire inlay on the stock

further improved by the thorough hammering and condensing of the iron. The iron used had first seen service in the shape of horseshoes and nails. A fanciful story is often repeated that the pounding of the iron on the roads gave it a special quality of toughness; however, any hardening induced in this manner would not have survived the bringing of the iron to white-hot temperature when the nails and shoes were forge welded together.

From around the middle of the eighteenth century English barrel-makers started to forge their barrels from long strips of iron made from imported horseshoe-nail stubs. These strips of iron, about three-quarters of an inch wide, were wound edge-to-edge in a spiral fashion round a steel mandrel. Next the iron was heated to white-hot welding temperature; the edges were then jumped together by banging down the end of the mandrel and welded with hammer blows on a U-shaped anvil. When the whole barrel had been welded, it was cold hammered to condense and toughen the metal thoroughly. The hollow tube was then bored out inside and filed down outside to the correct proportions. Because the grain of the high-quality iron went round the barrel it was better able to withstand the lateral stresses and so could be made lighter in weight. By the last quarter of the century most English guns were fitted with barrels of this type, usually known as 'stub twist'. They can be distinguished by the light- and dark-brown streaks that spiral the barrel; this pattern was brought out by the controlled rusting process known as 'browning' which both finishes and protects the metal.

Throughout the eighteenth century the style of shooting remained much the same. Birds such as partridges and grouse were walked up with the aid of pointers and setters, and the shots were almost all at birds flying directly away. Pheasants and woodcock would be flushed out by spaniels and also mostly shot going directly away. Duck were flushed up from ponds early in the season, and later in mid-winter stalked when on ponds with special big-bore long-barrelled duck guns, the idea being to shoot them on the water or better still the moment they lifted off. The slight delay between the flash of the powder in the pan and the firing of the main charge was just about right; as the duck lifted out of the water on seeing the flash they exposed the maximum target to the charge that followed.

Unlike some highly organized shoots in Europe, the British sportsman was content with modest bags. It was a matter of enjoying fresh air and healthy exercise alone with his dogs or with a few local friends, with the added pleasure of bringing home a few birds for the table or to present to neighbours.

The last quarter of the eighteenth century saw a number of improvements and changes in the sporting gun and also the emergence of a particularly English gun. The lock was improved by fitting a small wheel between the frizzen and its spring; this caused it to fly open more readily to expose the priming to the sparks. The friction between the mainspring and the tumbler was eliminated by the introduction of a steel swivel and the pan was made more proof against rain by cutting away the metal around it.

The introduction of Henry Nock's patent breech and other similar breeches caused the charge to be exploded more efficiently, thereby enabling the barrel to be shortened. Also helpful in this respect was the improvement in the

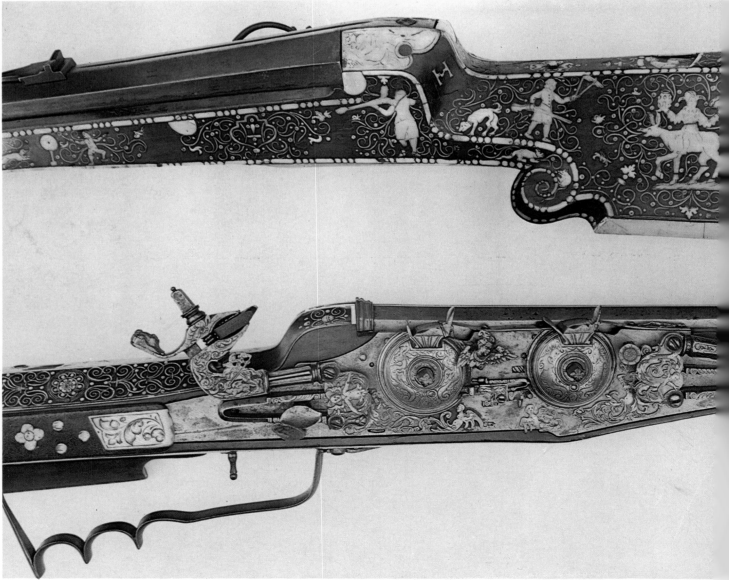

A fine-quality silver-mounted flintlock *Jäger* rifle by
Paul Poser of Prague, *c.* 1750

An English 10-bore double-barrelled big-game rifle made
by Charles Lancaster for the Maharajah of Jodhpur in
1863. It has heavily gilded locks and furniture and
fine-quality Damascus twist barrels.

A matchlock target rifle with bone inlay in the stock, from
southern Germany, *c.* 1580, *(top)* and a fine-quality
German wheel-lock rifle with two locks, designed to fire
superimposed loads from the same barrel, *c.* 1595 *(bottom)*

A French double-barrelled
flintlock sporting gun, dated
1797, by Cramont à
Bordeaux. It has silver
mounts, a stock inlaid with
silver wire and silver-plated
locks.

A mid eighteenth-century English silver-mounted fowling
piece by John Harman, London, with a Spanish barrel by
Francisco Bis of Madrid

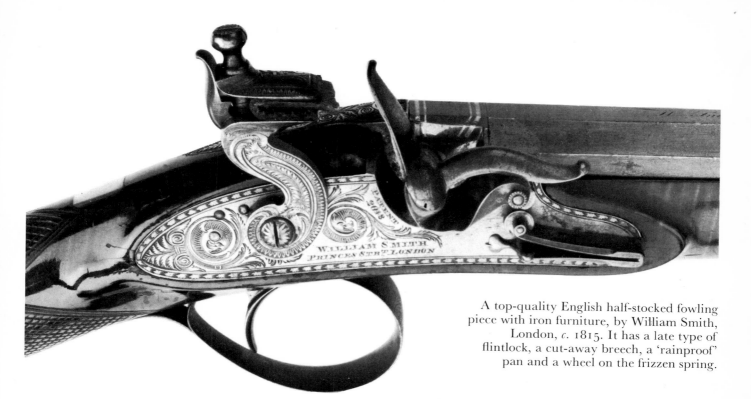

A top-quality English half-stocked fowling piece with iron furniture, by William Smith, London, *c.* 1815. It has a late type of flintlock, a cut-away breech, a 'rainproof' pan and a wheel on the frizzen spring.

quality of gunpowder. Shot also was improved in roundness, by pouring molten lead through a fine sieve from the top of a tall shot-tower into water below. It was then graded according to size: No. 9 or 8 for snipe, 7, 6 or 5 for general game, and 4, 3, 2 or 1 for duck and geese. The old method of sizing shot was in the following order, starting with the smallest: dust, mustard seed, cross, 1, 2, 3, 4, 5, 6, 7, 8 and then swan drops.

The sporting gun with its improved lock and shorter barrel was also distinguished by the half stock held to the barrel by two bolts and the use of lightly-engraved iron furniture. Although somewhat plain when compared to former silver-mounted guns, closer inspection showed its excellent functional qualities. This type of gun was the forerunner of the English style that was to be fully developed in the nineteenth century. The absence of carving and inlay in the stock allowed the natural beauty of the wood to be appreciated fully. Though a functional device, the chequering of the grip provided a decorative contrast to the polished surfaces. And of course the figure of the browned twist barrel had a subtle beauty of its own which greatly enhanced a fine gun.

In the second half of the eighteenth century a number of side-by-side double-barrelled guns were made. Even though the number being made increased in the last quarter, they were still much less common than the standard single guns. The use of lighter and shorter barrels did much to make these guns practicable. A few earlier guns had been made with the barrels set one on top of the other, operating on the turnover principle with one lock serving both barrels. It was the side-by-side arrangement with a rib between and a lock on each side that was to be the gun of the future.

Double guns were at first considered rather unsporting, one shot at a time being considered sufficient. Also it was thought that accidents were more likely with double guns. For this there was some justification: when only one barrel had been fired, it had to be charged with the hand over the other

loaded barrel. Again, if the shooter had neglected to set the cock down to safe at half cock, the ramming of the charge might jerk it from a lightly-held sear. Also there was the chance, in the heat of the moment, of accidentally double-charging the barrel that was already loaded.

Some indication of the date of an eighteenth-century gun can be gained from the design of the finiel in front of the trigger-guard. In the first half of the century a form of foliated trefoil was often used, and from about 1750 an acorn, which was replaced by a pineapple from about 1780. The pineapple motif was still in use in the 1860s.

In the first half of the century Barbar and Freeman were notable gunmakers, whereas in the second half Griffin, Bailes, Twigg and Durs Egg were famous names. Two of the most celebrated English gunmakers, the brothers John and Joseph Manton, set up in business in the last years of the century but the full flowering of their genius belongs to the first quarter of the nineteenth century when the double-barrelled sporting gun was perfected.

John Manton, after rising to the position of foreman with John Twigg, set up on his own in 1781. Joseph served his apprenticeship with his brother and went into business on his own account in 1789. Both brothers made a variety of fine weapons but Joseph applied his talents particularly to the double sporting gun. The ignition of the charge was speeded up by making the action of the cock shorter and sharper; the shape of the pan was improved and the touch-hole inset to bring it nearer to the centre of the breech. The locks were more closely set together, making the gun neater in appearance. As an aid to aiming, the barrels were mounted with an elevated rib so that the centre of the shot pattern was thrown above the point of aim. This enabled the shooter to keep a rising bird in view, instead of having to 'blot it out' when firing a little above it. The general style followed the tendency towards a functional gun with only light engraving on the

An English double-barrelled sporting gun by Joseph Manton, *c.* 1807. Half stocked with iron furniture, it has Manton's patent elevated rib.

Right: An early makeshift pigeon match about 1820, depicted in an aquatint by Henry Alken. The trapper, seated, pulls the box open with a cord to release the pigeon.

Below right: The Gun Club, Notting Hill, a photograph of the International Meeting 1894. In the centre, wearing a top hat, is James Purdey 'the Younger', who attended the meetings regularly to see to the interests of his customers, as did many leading gunmakers.

iron furniture for relief. However the clean graceful lines and perfection of fit and finish of all parts give these guns great character. They are the essence of the best tradition in British gunmaking.

The classic book of shooting, *Instructions to Young Sportsmen in all that relates to Guns and Shooting*, did much to arouse interest. It was written in 1814 by the lively and forthright Colonel Peter Hawker who was forever experimenting with guns and shooting, and in speech and writing he extolled the virtues of the guns built by his great friend, Joe Manton. Hawker's favourite game gun was fondly named 'Old Joe'. It was a 19-bore double gun that started life as a flintlock and was later converted to percussion with new breeches and locks. His favourite 5-bore duck gun, which weighed 19 pounds, he named 'Big Joe'.

Hawker, by his writing on the subject, did much to arouse interest in wildfowling on lonely stretches of salt marsh and in the creeks and channels around the coast. Previously this type of shooting had been left to local shoremen shooting for the pot and professional wildfowlers.

Though the flintlock had been improved, it still suffered some delay in igniting the main charge and it was also susceptible to rain or damp. However, a new system of ignition that was to be of tremendous importance in the development of the gun was patented in 1807 by Alexander Forsyth, a minister of Belhelvie in Scotland. The early system, which involved the use of detonating powder in a small magazine, was too complicated and expensive to be adopted generally. However a variety of ideas were tried out by other gunmakers, using the powder in pills, discs, tubes, tapes and caps. In the end it was the percussion cap, fitting on to a nipple screwed into the breech, that proved the most widely acceptable.

This was a great step forward, for the new ignition was almost instantaneous and although not entirely proof against rain it was very much more so than the flintlock. There was some controversy in the 1820s as to the rival merits of flint and percussion, but by the 1830s very few flintlock guns were being made or used. Many were in fact converted to percussion cap, by the cheap method of screwing a side plug containing a nipple in place of the touch-hole and replacing the cock with a hammer. The better method was to fit new breeches and new percussion locks because, in a double gun particularly, the nipple could be placed near the centre of the breech giving much better ignition. By the 1830s also, the double gun became the standard game gun. The typical example had 30-inch twist barrels, was half stocked with the fore end held by a single bolt and had iron furniture. It was neat, well balanced, simple to operate and reliable; it helped to give impetus to the growing interest in shooting, and coincided with the beginnings of serious game-preserving and the rearing of game birds.

Game was still almost entirely walked up in the old style, but with the almost instantaneous ignition of the percussion double gun it became possible for sportsmen to take shots at birds coming, going or crossing at any angle with a reasonable chance of success. This led to experiments in driving game over the heads of a line of guns, in particular the flushing of pheasants from specially-planted coverts.

It was increasingly the custom in the nineteenth century for best-quality guns to be sold in mahogany cases, together

with all the equipment needed for loading and cleaning. This was partly because it was customary for keen sportsmen to travel further afield for their sport. In the early nineteenth century many travelled by road to the Yorkshire moors in August for the grouse, but with the coming of the railways such travel was immensely increased.

Sporting landowners would invite each other to shoot on their estates and vie as to the numbers of game bagged. Queen Victoria and Prince Albert helped to make Scotland a fashionable sporting area, and many followed their example in buying shooting estates there.

Between the 1820s and 1860 the percussion gun changed little; in fact many sportsmen and gunmakers considered it the perfect gun and wished for nothing better. There were numbers of excellent gunmakers but two in particular, James Purdey and Charles Lancaster, carried on in the direct tradition of the Mantons, making superbly-finished functional guns devoid of any superfluous ornament except for discreet scroll-engraving on the locks and furniture.

The Great Exhibition of 1851 was destined to be the beginning of the end for the muzzle-loading sporting gun: it was there that the French gunmaker Lefaucheux exhibited his pin-fire breech-loading gun. Though relatively crude, it embodied the main principles of a practicable breech-loader. The gun opened at the breech in what is usually called the drop-down principle, allowing the brass and paper cartridge to be inserted. On being closed, the barrels were secured by a bolt that fitted into a slot in the projection or lump brased under the breech ends of the barrels. This bolt was operated by a lever set forward of the trigger-guard. An overhead hammer struck the pin projecting from the cartridge, firing the percussion cap inside. There was a small recess in the top breech ends of the barrels to allow for the projecting pin.

Joseph Lang has the credit for being the first English gunmaker to take up the idea. Within about a year he had brought out a much improved version. From then on numerous others took up the challenge, endeavouring by a variety of ingenious means to make the closure of the action more secure and simpler to operate. One of the strongest and widely-popular actions was the under-lever one, in which the barrels were firmly secured in a short screw movement on returning the lever from the side to its position under the trigger-guard. So strong was this action that it continued for many years for big-bore guns and heavy rifles. Other notable actions were the Dougall Lockfast, in which the barrels moved forward off the breech before hinging down, and two early snap actions, that is with bolts that automatically spring into place on closure of the gun. Westley Richards' gun was closed by a snap-action bolt that secured the 'doll's head' extension of the barrels to the top of the breech. James Purdey's snap action was operated by a thumb lever through an aperture in the front of the trigger-guard.

Far from being welcomed by the majority of sportsmen, these new pin-fire breech-loaders provoked a heated controversy which was aired in the sporting magazines of the day. At last, in 1858 and 1859, Mr Walsh, the editor of *The Field*, arranged trials between muzzle- and breech-loading guns. The muzzle-loaders won the contest—on the second occasion only by a narrow margin—and the breech-loaders used a quarter of a dram of powder more than the muzzle-loaders.

However, many sportsmen were convinced that the ease and safety of loading more than compensated for the slightly inferior shooting qualities. The breech-loader could not be double loaded and there was no longer the danger of a flask exploding when powder was poured, for example, onto a piece of tow in the breech that happened to be smouldering. The barrels could easily be looked through to check for any mud or snow that had got into them or to see that they had been thoroughly cleaned. Sore fingers from ramming charges down a fouled barrel and fumbling with the caps with frozen fingers were both avoided. So was the need to place the butt down on muddy ground to reload and the annoyance, when walking up in line, of having to wait for a shooter to rummage through his pockets looking for his powder, shot, wads and caps. A shooter with a breech-loader could keep moving forward as he loaded.

Percussion muzzle-loading guns continued to be made into the 1860s. However, the introduction by George Daw in 1861 of the centre-fire cartridge, patented by Pottet of Paris in 1855, soon swung the balance in favour of the breech-loader.

It should be mentioned here that a remarkable centre-fire gun and cartridge had been patented by Charles Lancaster in 1852. The gun embodied features that were new at the time, such as the cartridge-extractor arm that moved out as the barrels hinged down and the action that was operated by an arm that swung back under the trigger-guard. Lancaster's cartridge contained the detonating mixture between two sheets of brass at the rear end of the cartridge, the inner sheet being perforated by four holes. The cartridge was fired when a blunt pin through the breech face was struck by a hammer. Though this gun was well ahead of its time, its expense and the limitation of patent rights prevented it making much headway against the pin-fire. On the other hand George Daw failed to obtain exclusive patent right to the Pottet cartridge in England, enabling it to be readily adopted as a considerable improvement on the pin-fire.

In the 1860s and '70s the centre-fire breech-loader was immensely improved and rapidly replaced both the muzzle-loader and the pin-fire. In 1867 the Purdey bolt was patented. This double-bite snap action was at first operated by the thumb lever, but in the 1870s the familiar top lever was introduced. This bolt and lever is still the most widely used fastening for sporting guns. An improved version of the rebounding lock was patented in 1869; this was a great help because the hammer no longer needed to be pulled back to half cock to open the gun. Not only did the hammers rebound to half cock but also the strikers were sprung so that they returned behind the breech face allowing the gun to open freely.

Damascus barrels containing more steel were used at this time. The best Damascus barrels of this period were superb examples of the barrel-forgers' art and were stronger than the old stub twist because they contained steel as well as iron. One of the most common methods was to fire-weld together alternate strips of iron and steel into rods about a quarter of an inch square. These rods were then heated and tightly twisted, after which three of them were forged together into a strip about three-quarters of an inch wide. This was coiled in a spiral edge-to-edge round a mandrel and forged into a tube in the same manner as the stub-twist barrels formerly described. After finishing, these barrels were browned and the

A photograph of a group
of shooters with percussion guns,
c. 1850-60

Above: A pin-fire double-barrelled gun by John Dickson & Son, *c.* 1860, shown open with one cartridge partly out of the breech. The under-lever closes under the trigger-guard.

Below: Charles Lancaster's remarkable centre-fire gun and cartridge of 1852. The method of closure and the use of extractors were ahead of their time.

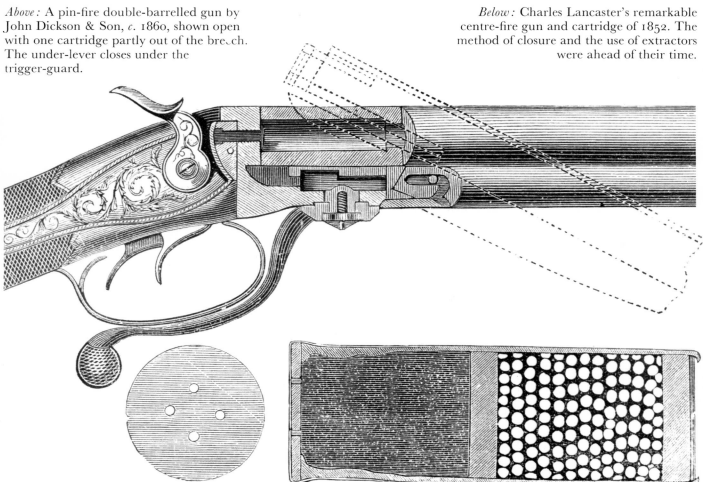

beautiful pattern of the alternate iron and steel is revealed in fine curls of light and dark brown.

For centuries gunmakers had tried various ways of boring barrels to make them throw the shot pattern both hard and close. One of the most common methods was to bore the barrel a little wider at the breech, then tight for most of its length, opening it slightly in the final few inches. In 1866 William Pape of Newcastle provisionally patented an idea for making a barrel shoot closely by choking or constricting the bore at the muzzle. He was awarded a prize as the inventor of choke boring in 1875. The idea of choke boring was taken up by a number of gunmakers in Britain and America, but the gunmaker who did most to perfect and publicize the idea was W. W. Greener of Birmingham. When W. W. Greener in 1874 advertized choke-bored guns capable of throwing regular and close patterns quite beyond anything heard of before, letters of disbelief poured in to the sporting magazines. Once again *The Field* stepped in, and in 1875 a comprehensive trial was arranged between cylinders and choke-bored barrels. The trial was conclusively won by W. W. Greener with a gun throwing an average of 214 pellets of No.6 shot in a 30-inch circle at 40 yards.

At last gunmakers had at their disposal the means of regulating a barrel to make it shoot close, but this was not the whole story. Many sportsmen, having tried tightly-choked guns for game shooting, found to their dismay that at the closer ranges the pattern was so close that they missed, where they would have hit with a cylinder, or the bird was hit by so many shot that it was unfit to eat.

Within a few years some sort of compromise was achieved, and the average game gun was bored with a slight degree of choke in the right barrel and in the left the choke was modified to about half full-choke. Naturally in guns designed for specific purposes such as wildfowling, where longer ranges would be expected, much more choke was used.

One result of choke boring was to make smaller charges of shot at least as effective as heavier charges had been in a cylinder. The use of lighter loads enabled guns to be made lighter, though 30 inches was to remain the standard length for barrels well into the twentieth century.

The hammer gun had hardly been perfected when the restless energy of gunmakers turned to the design of guns with the 'hammers' inside the lock, the guns being usually termed 'hammerless'. The first of these to achieve reasonable success was Murcott's, patented in 1871, in which the barrels were released and the 'hammers' cocked on thrusting down the lever under the trigger-guard. Of the others that followed, the Anson and Deeley was one of the most important for it formed the basis of all boxlock guns, in which the pins of both locks extend through the action body. In Westley Richards' Anson and Deeley action, brought out in 1875, the fall of the barrels was utilized to cock the hammers, a method that quickly replaced the lever system.

Of the sidelock hammerless guns, one of the finest and most graceful in appearance was the one made by J. Purdey, patented by Frederick Beesley in 1880. In this gun the mainspring was cleverly utilized to assist the opening of the gun. Also, because the springs were only put under full tension when the barrels were closed, they were released when the gun was put away in its case.

With an efficient hammerless gun it might be thought that gunmakers and sportsmen would rest content for a while. Soon, however, gunmakers set about devising patent ejectors that would throw the fired cartridges clear when the gun was opened. One of the first was designed by J. Needham in 1874, and Deeley added a good one to the Anson and Deeley gun in 1886. By the 1890s they had become reliable and their use general.

Of considerable importance in the history of sporting shooting was the invention of various types of smokeless or nitro powder. One of the first of these to oust black powder was a nitro-wood compound named Schultze, after the inventor, a Prussian artillery officer. After a number of early difficulties, and accidents caused by the very high pressures given by some of the early nitro powders, their use had become general by about 1890. The absence of smoke had the advantage that the second barrel could be fired quickly without the vision being obscured.

Single-trigger mechanisms were brought out by many leading gunmakers in the 1890s, one of the earliest successes being by John Robertson, the proprietor of Boss and Company. Steel barrels began to replace Damascus barrels from the 1880s and '90s, the first being the fine but expensive Whitworth steel barrels.

The basic designs of sporting guns and cartridges have changed little in the twentieth century. A sidelock or boxlock hammerless ejector gun made in the 1890s hardly differs from a recently-made gun. There has, however, been a tendency to lighter guns and shorter barrels: good examples of such guns being the well-known Churchill XXV with its 25-inch barrels and the Lancaster 'Twelve-Twenty', a 12-bore gun made as light as a normal 20-bore. Also in the twentieth century there was a return to the over-and-under arrangement of barrels and this still remains popular in some quarters for game shooting. Woodward's over-and-under gun was a very fine example of this type. They are, incidentally, more expensive to make than side-by-side guns of equivalent quality.

With the coming of breech-loaders there was also a considerable change in the style and scale of shooting. Tendencies towards more rearing and driving of game birds were greatly accelerated in the second half of the nineteenth century. Shooting estates and shooters became more and more conscious of the numbers of game bagged, competing with each other to this end. Estates that had formerly been shot over by the owner and a few local friends tended to be the scene of shooting house-parties to which the notable shots of the day were invited. Two of the finest, Lord Ripon and Lord Walsingham, often shot six days a week and counted their bags in thousands. Every endeavour was made to test shooting skill, for instance by driving pheasants over the shooters' heads very high and fast. In fact, skill with the gun to a great extent replaced the enjoyment of walking-up game, in which fieldcraft, robust exercise, the observation of nature, good company and the pleasure of working dogs was as much to be appreciated as marksmanship. Even Lord Ripon looked back nostalgically to the simpler pleasures of his early shooting days.

Two World Wars have broken up or impoverished the great shooting estates. Shoots are now largely controlled by syndicates which are joined at so much per gun per annum, according to the quality of the shooting provided. Pigeon shooting and rough shooting still offer sport for those less affluent. Wildfowling on the salt marshes, traditionally a free sport testing in endurance and perseverance, has recently been largely managed by wildfowling clubs.

One aspect of shooting that has become increasingly popular in recent years is the sport of shooting 'clays'. These targets, like small flying-saucers, are flung at a variety of angles which test the skill of the shooter and break into a puff of dust in the most satisfying manner when truly hit.

This sport had its beginnings in the early years of the nineteenth century when a few shooters would gather together to test their skill on pigeon released from 'traps'. The pigeon had to be 'grassed' within a set boundary. Often these pigeon matches took place beside a country public-house. The 'Old Hats' at Ealing is thought to have got its name from the use of hats over holes in the ground as makeshift traps, the hats being pulled away by a long cord to release the bird.

As the sport grew, valuable prizes were offered and there was a great deal of gambling on shooters. Special single-barrel guns were soon made of big bore to take heavy loads of shot, and all sorts of irregular and unfair practices tended to creep in. At an intermediate stage, attempts were made to regularize the sport with a set of stringent rules and the limitation of guns to below 11 bore, firing no more than $1\frac{1}{4}$ ounces of shot. Such clubs as the 'Red House' and 'Hornsey Wood House' gave place towards the end of the century to strict, well-run clubs like 'The Gun Club', Notting Hill, and the 'Hurlingham Gun Club'. These clubs were attended by the leading gun-, shot- and powder-makers, all anxious to secure the patronage of the best shots so that their products could be seen to be successful. The standard type of pigeon gun was now a 12-bore double-barrelled gun, heavier than a game gun and designed to fire $1\frac{1}{4}$ ounces of shot. Percussion-cap muzzle-loaders were used for trap-pigeon shooting into the 1870s, usually without provision for a ramrod (a loading rod being used instead). However, when centre-fire hammer and later hammerless guns became reliable, these were used in preference. Most of these guns too were heavier than a game gun with a considerable degree of choke in the barrels and a raised rib to make them shoot high of the mark, so that the rising bird could be kept in view.

There were many pigeon clubs in Europe and America, one of the most famous being at Monaco where the great international meeting for the Grand Prix de Monte Carlo was held. In the 1880s two professional pigeon shooters arrived in Britain from America, each claiming to be champion of the world. First Captain Bogardus and then Dr Carver swept all before them with their new dedicated attitude. However Bogardus was eventually beaten by Mr Dudley Ward and Dr Carver held to a draw by Mr Stuart-Wortley in a match in which each had staked £500.

Live-pigeon shooting in Britain declined after 1900 and was later made illegal. However, from the 1880s there was increasing interest in the use of clay targets thrown from spring-loaded 'traps'. In Britain, these were mostly used for practice game-bird shooting in the new shooting schools established by leading gunmakers, but some early clay-pigeon clubs were formed. In America, shooting clays had

Driven-partridge shooting with pairs of centre-fire hammer or hammerless guns c. 1885. The loader kneels behind the shooter.

One of a pair of bar-in-wood centre-fire hammer guns by James Purdey & Sons, 1879. It has rebounding locks and top-lever snap-action fastening, and its fine Damascus twist barrels are bored to a modified choke.

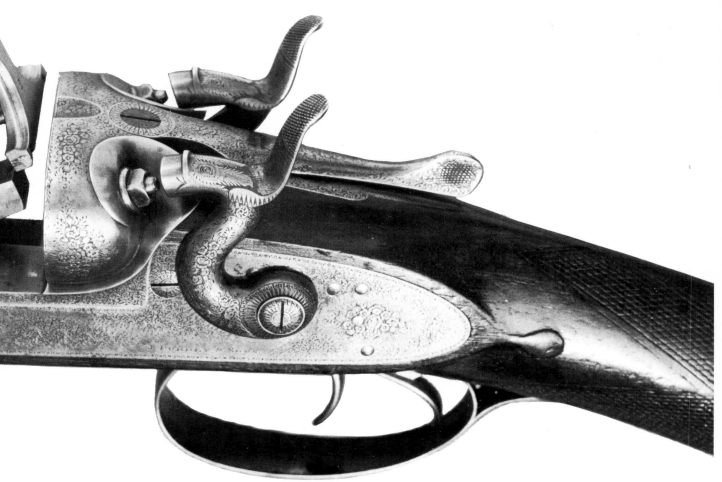

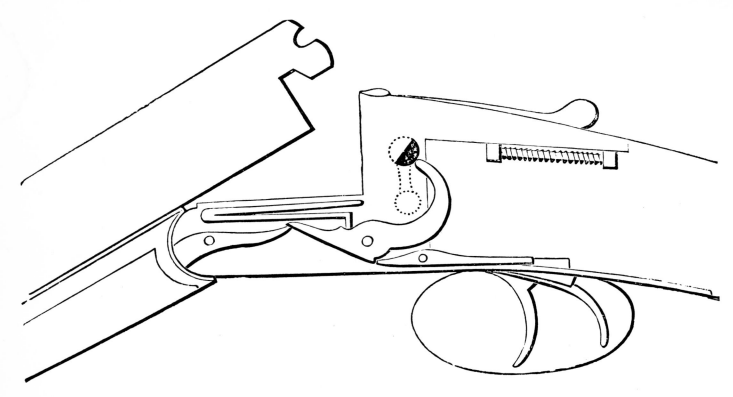

The original form of the famous Anson and Deeley
hammerless action, where the tumblers are cocked
on the fall of the barrels. This is a particularly strong
action which is notable for its economy of parts. It
was first produced by Westley Richards,
Birmingham, in 1876 and almost all modern
boxlock guns are based on this model.

A sidelock hammerless ejector gun by W. & C. Scott and Son,
the sporting-gun side of Webley and Scott Limited, c. 1922

Bob Braithwaite, winner of the Gold Medal for Olympic Trench Clay Pigeon Shooting at the Olympic Games in Mexico City, 1968. He is shooting with an over-and-under gun with a raised and ventilated top rib, typical of those most used for this sport.

become a sport in itself, and there were reports of up to 150 clays being broken in a straight run.

Today the most popular types of clay competition are 'Down the Line', clays going away at a variety of angles, and 'Skeet', clays crossing at various angles, the shooters moving round to different stations in turn to increase the variety of shots. Sporting shoots are also popular, and in these the clays are used to simulate the flight of various game birds in natural surroundings.

A great boost was recently given to British clay-pigeon shooting when J. R. Braithwaite won a gold medal for clay shooting at the Mexico Olympic Games in 1968.

The most popular clay guns today are the over-and-under type fitted with a top rib. These are made light and open bored for 'Skeet', and heavier, with more choke, for 'Down the Line' and 'Olympic Trench'. Special competition cartridges have been developed, using plastic cases, plastic cup-wads to protect the shot and very hard shot, the idea being to give patterns of shot that are as even as possible so that the 'clay' does not escape through a gap in the pattern.

Returning to look at the development of the sporting rifle in the eighteenth century, one finds that a characteristic hunting or *Jäger* rifle had evolved in Germany. Typically this rifle has a heavy, octagonal barrel with deep multigroove rifling and a shoulder stock with a cheekpiece and a sliding wooden patchbox. The wheel-lock was so well liked in Germany that it continued to be used into the eighteenth century, when it was replaced by a flintlock. These rifles were designed to take a tightly-patched ball which needed considerable effort to force it down the barrel. They were well suited to the type of forest and mountain hunting for which they were intended, being capable of delivering a heavy ball with great accuracy.

The few rifles that were required in the eighteenth century in Britain for use in deer parks were modelled on the flintlock version of the German hunting rifle. They had the typical heavy octagonal barrel and butt with a cheekpiece and sliding wooden patchbox cover. Towards the end of the century they were distinguished by the half stock and the plain but graceful finish of the sporting guns of that date. Fresh impetus was given to the British sporting rifle in the nineteenth century when the wonderful deer-stalking country of Scotland became easily accessible by rail. Also for officers serving abroad, explorers and hunters, undreamed-of opportunities opened up to encounter a great variety of game, and in particular the big game animals of Africa and India.

The typical percussion-cap deer-stalking rifle remained much the same as the flintlock rifles of the early nineteenth century, except that a circular patchbox was fitted. The standard size of bore was 16, firing a 1-ounce patched ball. These multigroove rifles were very accurate and had sufficient range and velocity for deer stalking. However, when hunters used these against larger or more dangerous animals, they soon discovered their inadequacy, especially in velocity. If they increased the powder charge beyond what was very moderate ($1\frac{1}{2}$ drams was usual with a 1-ounce ball), the ball was liable to strip across the rifling and have no more accuracy than a smooth bore. In fact, as some of the larger animals were shot at close range, many hunters took to using smooth-bore guns designed for very powerful charges and in some cases hunters even had their rifles bored out smooth.

William Cotton Oswell, who accompanied David Livingstone on some of his expeditions, did most of his hunting with a double-barrelled 10-bore ball gun firing 6 drams of fine-grain powder. As he mostly hunted in the saddle, running his quarry and bringing it to bay, this smooth-bore gun had sufficient accuracy. It also had great velocity, coupled with a heavy ball, and gave him two chances. Because it was a smooth bore it was easier to load while in the saddle. It proved very effective, even against elephant, one or two balls usually proving sufficient.

For those hunters who required accuracy and high velocity, the two-groove rifle proved most useful. It employed either a ball cast with a raised belt that exactly fitted the grooves or a conical bullet with projections on either side that also keyed exactly into the rifling.

The famous hunter Samuel White-Baker was one of the first to have such a rifle made to his specifications in the 1840s. It weighed 22 pounds and carried a belted ball of 3 ounces and a conical bullet of 4 ounces, propelled by 16 drams of powder. This tremendous rifle proved to be extremely effective and more than once saved Baker from the most determined charges of elephant or buffalo.

Hunters confronted with dangerous animals often had desperate need of a second quick shot, so the double rifle was developed on much the same lines as the shotgun. Very great skill was needed to align the two rifle barrels to shoot accurately to the one pair of sights along the rib.

A hunting expedition, in southern Africa for instance, was fraught with difficulties and danger of which hunters in recent times can have little conception. There was the need to carry in ox waggons supplies and ammunition for months and sometimes years, trekking over country few or no Europeans had ever seen before. The crossing of rivers entailed a risk of getting stuck or being swept away; there was the possibility of injury, illness and fever to men, horses and oxen. Also tribal wars sometimes made things even more difficult.

Of course, in the days of the muzzle-loader the hunting itself presented many hazards. Imagine the desperate efforts to ram home a sticking ball as a furious lion or buffalo was about to charge. Or the awful feeling when one pulled the trigger in a tight situation, heard the dull click of the hammer, and realized that the cap had missed fire or fallen off. Then there was the period when the smoke from the first shot obscured a charging beast, causing moments of suspense until either it was close upon the hunter or appeared disabled through the clearing smoke at a short distance.

On return to camp all the barrels had to be washed through, dried and lightly oiled; also the nipple and hammer cup had to be cleaned. Any fouling left in the breech or nipple, or too much oil, could cause a misfire on the morrow in very awkward circumstances.

Though there were obvious advantages in breech-loading rifles, not least the ability to reload quickly in an emergency, they were not much used in the 1850s and '60s. This was mainly because the breech pressures were much higher in heavy rifles and the early actions were not strong enough to withstand them.

Muzzle-loading rifles were still being made in the 1860s. The well-known ivory hunter Frederick Courtney Selous

A Webley and Scott
over-and-under gun with a
raised and ventilated rib
and a pistol grip, specially
designed for 'clay' shooting.

Two German
seventeenth-century
wheel-lock rifles of fine
quality, the one on the
left being a light birding
rifle or *tschinke*

An English percussion cap deer-stalking rifle made by William Moore for the Earl of Dunmore, c. 1840

Deer stalking amid the grandeur of the Scottish hills. An engraving from *The Art of Deerstalking* by William Scrope, 1838.

brought breech-loading deer rifles with him to southern Africa in 1871 but did all his early elephant shooting with 4-bore muzzle-loaders. These 4-bore guns were cheap Birmingham-made duck guns sold for £6 in Africa. With a handful of coarse powder and a 4-ounce ball they were tremendously effective at close range. Selous would keep up a running battle with the elephants, pursuing them on foot, and shooting and reloading as he ran. When charged he would run for it until able to reload and return to do battle again.

By the 1880s strong and efficient breech-loading centre-fire hammer rifles and brass-cased cartridges were being used in preference to muzzle-loaders. There were so many advantages to breech-loaders that the life of a hunter was made easier and safer. It was wonderful to be able to load so quickly, with no percussion cap to be put on, no ball to stick in the barrel, no breech and nipple to foul up and much easier cleaning. Also, because a breech-loader could be so quickly

reloaded, there was not the need to have spare guns carried by gun bearers as the tiger-shooter Lieutenant Rice had done. He and his companions in India often set out with three double rifles each.

Breech-loaders were not only safer because a hunter could reload more quickly. The danger of not being able to ram the ball right down on the powder was liable to be very serious too. Gordon Cumming twice had rifles blow up when in pursuit of elephants. Almost certainly this was because he did not notice in the heat of the moment that the bullet was not right down on the powder. Incidentally, Selous was once knocked backwards and badly shaken when his African servant accidentally double loaded one of his 4-bore guns.

In the 1880s and '90s came the change to smokeless nitro powders, the use of smaller-calibre elongated bullets and concentration on high velocity. It was soon found that high-velocity elongated bullets had to be designed to expand in the

A big-game rifle made by Charles Lancaster, 1863, shown
in its baize-lined oak case with equipment including
bullet mould, powder flask, patch cutter, patchbox, nipple
key, powder measure, percussion caps, bullets, cleaning
rod and jags, mops and wire brushes.

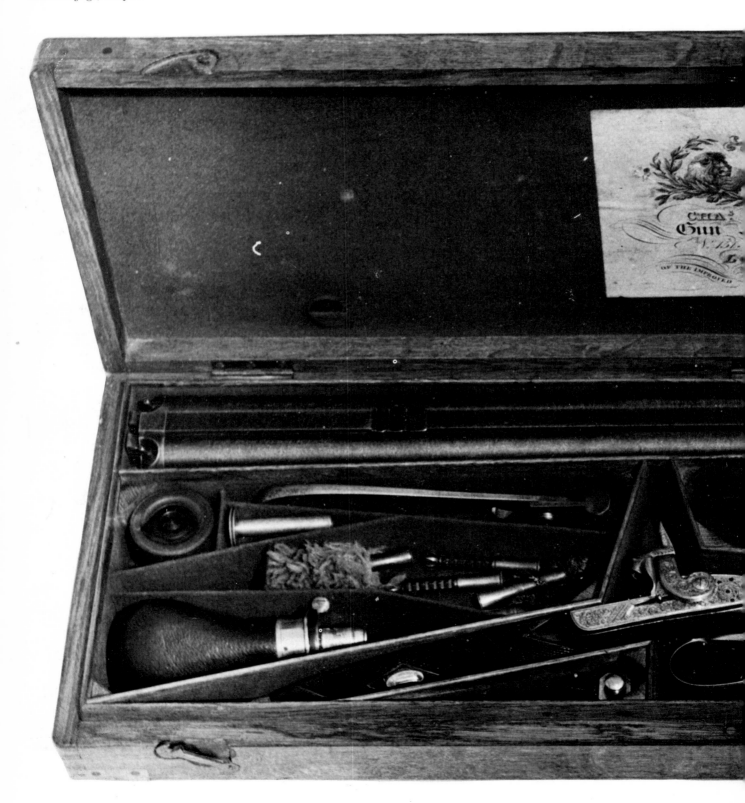

A double-barrelled 4-bore hammer rifle by Daniel Frazer of Edinburgh, *c.* 1880

Sir Henry Morton Stanley, the explorer, photographed in the clothes he wore when he met David Livingstone near Lake Tanganyika in 1871. He carries a double-barrelled percussion-cap muzzle-loading rifle. With him is his adopted African son.

animal's body if they were to achieve the maximum effect.

Nitro powders, and especially cordite, were found to corrode barrels badly, particularly Damascus barrels. This accelerated the change over to steel, which resisted corrosion better. Where extremes of climate were met some sportsmen preferred to use black powder, which could be relied upon to remain stable under almost any conditions.

By 1900 the hunter had the choice of a superb range of high-velocity rifles of a variety of bores and cartridges designed for all types of game. Nitro powders had become more reliable and both single and double rifles were made in hammerless sidelock or boxlock and fitted with ejectors. Bolt-action magazine rifles were also made, often based on the Mauser or Mannlicher designs, and the falling-block mechanisms were very popular for single-shot stalking and target rifles, especially the Gibbs-Farquharson with Metford rifling. The Gibbs-Metford .461 was F. C. Selous's favourite rifle during his last twelve years in Africa at the end of the century.

The ball gun was perfected into the very useful ball and shot gun invented by Colonel Fosbery, VC. This gun was similar to a shotgun except that the last few inches of each barrel were rifled, a device which enabled a ball or conical channelured bullet to be shot with accuracy at 100 yards. It was made by Holland and Holland in bores ranging from 8 to 20. The bigger bores were capable of dealing with the largest of animals and could also be used as shotguns. They were therefore ideal in country where a variety of game, large and small, might be encountered and of course were excellent for 'filling the pot'.

The 4- and 8-bore guns tended to go out of favour and to be replaced by the .577 or .500 Express or something like the Rigby .450 special with a muzzle velocity of 2,050 feet per second.

Deer stalkers took to the .303 rifle, firing a cartridge similar to the military one but with a soft-nosed bullet. These stalking rifles were now often fitted with telescopic sights.

Popular for rook and rabbit shooting were a variety of light single-barrelled hammer and hammerless rifles firing low-velocity cartridges with a ball or shot bullet of about .300 calibre. These very attractive rifles were, however, soon to be replaced by the .22 which also became the standard for miniature rifle-shooting on the 25-yard range.

The most generally-used stalking rifles today are of the bolt-action magazine type, fitted with telescopic sights, in bores less than .300 but with very high velocity. The advantages of very high velocity are the tremendous shock imparted by a suitably-designed bullet and the low trajectory of the bullet, a great assistance in aiming because shots will be near enough on the same mark at 50, 100 and 150 yards.

The finest double hammerless ejector rifles are still made for big game in bores that range from .577 to the smaller bores.

The whole character of big-game hunting has changed out of all recognition from the robust early days of the mighty hunters and their muzzle-loaders. Between the two World Wars railways and elaborately-equipped motorized safaris brought the hunter to the big game of Africa and professional 'white hunters' took the man who could pay to the 'trophy' he wished to shoot. Since 1945 the use of light aeroplanes to take the would-be 'hunter' within easy reach of the game has made travelling easy. Big-game shooting is now strictly controlled by the issue of licences to shoot each type of animal and by the supervision of official game wardens and hunters.

Though the hunting of lesser animals is somewhat freer, it is also controlled in most countries. For the most part, sport must be hired by the day, week or season and carried out under supervision. Such sporting facilities now form an important part of the tourist and holiday industry of countries that are fortunate in possessing vast stretches of natural landscape rich in game. To those immersed in the day-to-day toil of big cities, a temporary escape to the pursuit of game in wild places gives release to the spirit in the fulfilment of man's ancient hunting instinct.

A hunter with a double-barrelled 8-bore hammerless rifle stands beside his rhino, *c.* 1910.

Officers of the 93rd, the Sutherland Highlanders, in shikar costumes with their percussion rifles and trophies, India, *c.* 1864. Officers serving in India enjoyed splendid opportunities for hunting big and small game.

A modern stalking rifle by Churchill Limited, London. This de-luxe quality Mauser-action rifle has a magazine for four cartridges and a Pfeiffer 'scope with Redfield mounts. It is produced in numerous calibres from .22/250 Remington to .308 (7.62 mm) Winchester.

Guns of the American West

The early settlers in America used muskets that they had brought with them, or that were later imported from Europe, for protection against bands of marauding Indians. These muskets were also employed for shooting deer and other game and probably used with shot instead of ball for bird shooting. A number of fowling pieces of various sizes were, no doubt, not only used for bird shooting but also loaded with ball for larger animals and, when need arose, for Indians. Possibly a few rifles were also brought or imported into America in the early days.

Sometime around the beginning of the eighteenth century, German and Swiss immigrants settled in various colonies, but particularly in Pennsylvania. They brought with them typical German hunting rifles, and there were amongst them gun-makers who began making this type of rifle. Gradually these were adapted to meet the needs of the frontiersmen and a particular style of American rifle evolved. The typical octagonal barrel was maintained, but it was lengthened considerably to around forty-five inches and the bore was reduced to take a smaller ball. The full stock was usually of ripple or curly maple, giving an alternate light and dark striped effect.

A white trapper armed with a flintlock gun or rifle. By Frederic Remington.

A notable characteristic was the pronounced bend of the slender butt, which was fitted with a patchbox on one side while a cheekpiece was carved on the other side. Though a sliding wooden patchbox was used on early models, this was soon replaced by the typical hinged brass type. The flintlocks for these rifles were usually imported from England or Germany.

By the War of Independence (1775–81) the typical American long rifle had evolved. It was of great value in the hands of those frontiersmen accustomed to its use for shooting game or in brushes with Indians. Familiar with the country and used to making full use of cover, these riflemen had a tremendous advantage over the closely-packed ranks of British redcoats armed with muskets.

It seems that the term 'Kentucky rifle' was first used during this war and, because it sounded well, soon came to be widely accepted, although the rifle was not made in Kentucky. The Kentucky rifle was ideally suited to the needs of the frontiersmen. The smaller bore enabled more bullets to be carried for the same weight and these could be easily loaded by the use of a greased cloth or leather patch, unlike the ball in the original

Left: The early style of the flintlock Pennsylvanian or 'Kentucky' rifle, having the typical sliding wooden patchbox of the German hunting rifles, *c.* 1760

A typical flintlock Kentucky rifle with a brass-hinged patchbox and a butt plate curved to fit the shoulder, *c.* 1800

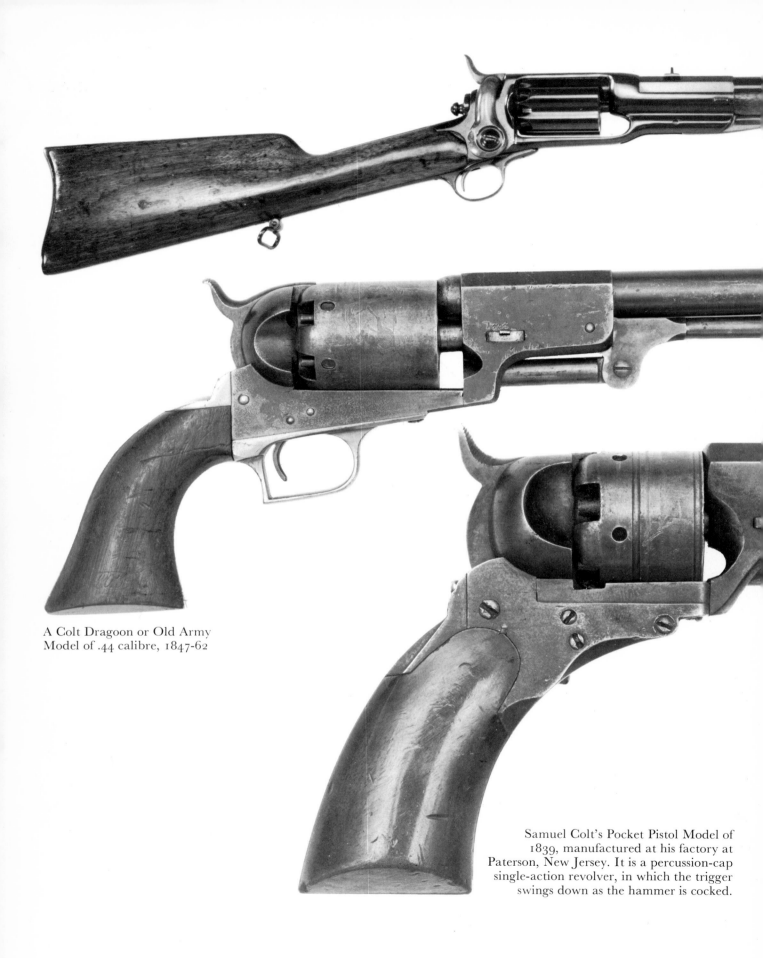

A Colt Dragoon or Old Army
Model of .44 calibre, 1847-62

Samuel Colt's Pocket Pistol Model of
1839, manufactured at his factory at
Paterson, New Jersey. It is a percussion-cap
single-action revolver, in which the trigger
swings down as the hammer is cocked.

Colt's revolving percussion-cap rifle. It has a side hammer and is full stocked, *c*. 1850.

Indians attacking a party of trappers who are loading and firing their flintlock guns, *c*. 1800. The figure in the foreground holds his ramrod in his hand to speed up reloading. A painting by Frederic Remington.

The famous single-action Army Model of 1873, otherwise known as the Frontier Model or the 'Peacemaker'

German rifle that had to be forcibly rammed. The slow-burning colonial-quality powder was suited to the progressive propulsion of the patched ball down a long barrel. The rifles therefore had a good velocity combined with great accuracy. Aiming too was assisted by the long heavy barrel, which gave steadiness and a good distance between the sights.

In the late eighteenth and first half of the nineteenth century the Kentucky rifle was refined and enriched with elaborately pierced and engraved brass or silver ornament. Especially elaborate patchboxes were inset into the butts and a variety of stars, eagles and other motifs were inlaid into the stocks. Percussion locks, of course, replaced the flintlocks in the nineteenth century. These percussion rifles were mainly used for hunting and target purposes. They were made in a variety of bores, later ones often being highly decorated.

The invention of the percussion cap made multi-shot weapons practical. The first weapons to be widely successful were the multi-shot pistols generally known as 'pepperboxes'. These pistols usually had from four to six barrels which were turned as the trigger was pulled, the trigger pull also cocking and releasing the hammer. This arrangement is known as a double action. Ethan Allen patented a pepperbox pistol in America in 1837. As a close-range self-protection weapon it was most effective, but, as it could not be aimed with any accuracy, it was limited to this rôle.

Samuel Colt was destined to be the man who invented and manufactured a series of revolving pistols sufficiently accurate, reliable and cheap to fill the needs of the Western frontier. But in spite of his later success things did not go too well for Colt in the early days. His first venture in manufacturing his single-action revolvers (patented in America in 1836) came to an end when his company, at Paterson, New Jersey, failed in 1843 for lack of orders.

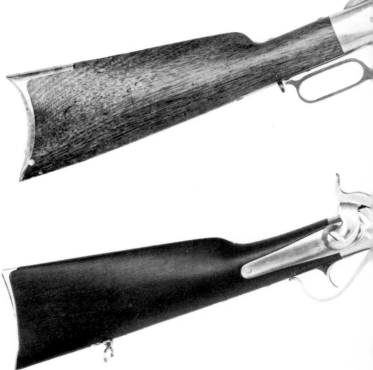

However, sufficient of Colt's revolvers had got into circulation for their worth to be established. Texas Rangers armed with Paterson Colts had defeated a far larger force of Comanches, and the revolver had proved particularly suited for use in a running fight on horseback. As a result Captain Walker, an officer with the United States Dragoons in Texas, was sent to persuade Colt to go back into business. Not only did he succeed in this, but he also helped in the design of a stronger and more powerful revolver, the .44-calibre Walker Colt of 1847, manufactured by Eli Whitney in his factory at Whitneyville, Connecticut.

The Mexican War of 1845–8 and the United States Army's orders for the Dragoon Colt, or Old Army Model, enabled Colt to set up on his own in a new factory at Hartford, Connecticut, in 1848. The United States Army was the first to issue its troops with revolvers, some 21,000 of the Old Army Model being produced from 1848 and some 200,000 of the New Army Model from 1860 to 1872. Several other models were made, the various pocket models, mostly in .31 calibre, and the .36-calibre navy models being extremely popular. Colt also applied his revolving principle to rifles and carbines, but these never achieved anywhere near the popularity of his revolvers. He was the first man to apply mass-production methods to firearms and from a military point of view the interchangeability of parts was an important advance.

After the war between the North and South (1861–5), there were a number of conversions to take cartridges. Then came the famous Single-Action Army Model of 1873, otherwise known as the Frontier Model or Peacemaker. Vast numbers of this type were produced in a variety of calibres and lengths of barrels; it was the most popular weapon associated with the great expansion westwards. The first double-action cartridge model, known as the Lightning Model, was not introduced until 1877. It was followed by the Double-Action Army or Frontier Model of 1878.

There were, of course, revolvers to rival the Colts, but they were not produced in anything like the same numbers. Of particular note are those produced by Remington and Smith and Wesson, these being strongly constructed with a solid frame enclosing the chambers.

Important in that it was to lead the way to repeating rifles was Walter Hunt's Volitional Repeater of 1849, in which his patent primed bullets were fed into the breech from a spring-loaded tubular magazine under the barrel. The invention by Benjamin Henry of a .44-calibre rim-fire metallic cartridge in 1860 resulted, after various improvements, in the famous Henry rifle. This was further improved in 1866 by the incorporation of Nelson King's side-gate loading system and was named the Winchester Repeating Rifle after the president of the company.

The chief rival of the Winchester was the Spencer Repeating Rifle, with a magazine in the butt. However, as the magazine carried seven cartridges to the Winchester's fifteen and as the hammer had to be cocked separately, it was not able to compete successfully. The Winchester Repeater, with its brass frame and lever behind the trigger-guard, was tremendously popular. A second model was brought out in 1873. It was designed to take centre-fire cartridges in a variety of calibres and a steel frame replaced the brass one.

The rifle was particularly suited to use from the saddle. Armed with a Winchester and a pair of Colts, a Westerner had the ideal armament to take on Indians in the sort of skirmishing, running fight at which they excelled in open country. The Winchester has been described as 'the gun that won the West', and there can be no doubt that it weighted the odds in favour of those who possessed them.

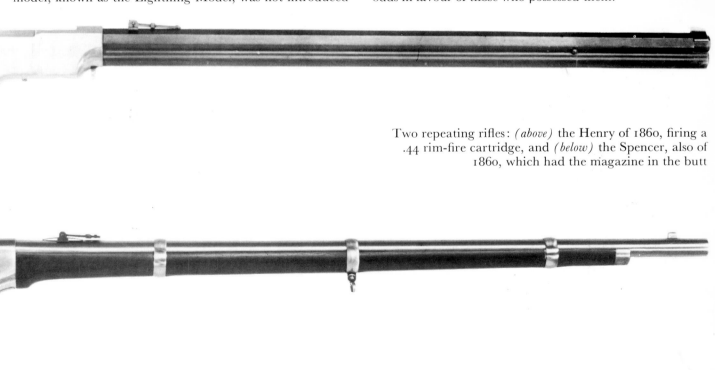

Two repeating rifles: *(above)* the Henry of 1860, firing a .44 rim-fire cartridge, and *(below)* the Spencer, also of 1860, which had the magazine in the butt

The Sharps capping breech-loaders, and in particular the vertical-breech carbine, had proved reliable and accurate in the Civil War. After the war many were converted to take metallic cartridges and there followed later models designed for cartridges. Of the converted rifles, the .50 was popular with buffalo hunters, and this was followed in 1874 by a rifle sometimes called the 'Sharps Buffalo Rifle'. This rifle, with a heavy octagonal barrel, was made in .50, .45 and smaller calibres.

The buffalo-hide hunters worked in small teams, the hunter having from two to five skinners according to his skill. The hunter would shoot from a fairly long range so that the buffalo would not be alarmed by the noise of the rifle and stampede. In this way the hunters were often able to shoot large numbers from a single stand. On one occasion a hunter, using two rifles, killed 120 in forty minutes; the record bag was 204. The skinners were kept very busy after the shoot. It was an unpleasant job for in hot weather there was soon a nauseating stench from carcases and hides. It is said that their trousers became so caked in dried blood and grease that they could be stood up on their own like a couple of drain pipes.

The Sharps rifles gained a reputation for accuracy at extraordinarily long ranges. An instance is recorded of an attack in 1874 by a large force of Comanches and southern Cheyennes under the half-white chief Quanah Parker on a small supply-centre in the heart of the Texas buffalo country. Among the twenty-seven men inside the fortified centre there were a number of buffalo hunters, including one of the greatest marksmen of the plains, Billy Dixon. The Indians were held at bay for four days by the accurate long-range fire of the

hunters, but when on the fourth day Billy Dixon shot one of them from his horse at a distance, later measured, of 1,385 yards they decided to move on. Dixon used one of the heavy .50 Sharps rifles for this extraordinary feat. A year later he killed another Indian at a mile distance when firing from a town under siege in Kansas.

While acting as an army scout, Dixon and four cavalrymen were caught on the open plains by a band of Indians. One of the cavalrymen was fatally wounded, but Dixon and the others managed to reach a buffalo wallow. By their deadly fire they kept the Indians from getting near enough to overrun them and at the same time they were able to scrape the wallow a bit deeper. The heat was terrific but they kept up their accurate fire until the remainder of the Indians departed to look for easier prey. The men concerned all received the Congressional Medal of Honour.

In 1878 the Sharps Rifle Company, at their new Bridgeport factory, brought out their superb sporting and target rifle with the hammerless action designed by Hugo Borchardt. This rifle was made in a number of models, including a .45 military type.

In the 1870s and '80s came the great Western expansion. It was the pioneering age of the railroads, of the waggon trains from the railroad onward, and the vast cattle-drives to the railhead towns. In these towns congregated cowboys, railmen, settlers, prospectors, adventurers, outlaws, gamblers and sometimes lawmen. The 'law' in such frontier towns consisted of a marshal who could use his guns well and was quick to do so. When cowpunchers, paid off after weeks on the trail, 'hit' town determined on hard drinking and having some fun,

The 1873 Model Winchester repeater designed for centre-fire cartridges and made in various calibres. In this model a steel frame replaced the brass frame of the earlier 1866 model.

An extra fine quality Model 1876 Winchester: an example of the famous 'One of a Thousand', said to be perfect in every respect

A Sharps Buffalo rifle with its characteristic heavy octagonal barrel. Made in .50, .45 and some smaller calibres, it was first introduced in 1874.

things often got out of hand. Drunken brawls ended in gun-fights or cowboys started to shoot up anything that would break. The system adopted by some of the early marshals of notorious Dodge City, for instance, was to shoot the ring-leaders, the six-gun being judge, jury and executioner.

These were rough-and-ready methods but if the marshal did not shoot first he was liable to be shot himself. As soon as a marshal got a reputation there was always some trigger-happy glory hunter ready to try and gun him down. When dealing with outlaws and gunmen a double-barrelled shotgun loaded with buckshot was sometimes used. Those marshals who relied on a fast draw soon found someone faster. Ed Masterson, Marshal of Dodge City, once went to deal with a Texan who had been 'raising hell' in one of the saloons. He asked the Texan to hand over his guns and immediately received two bullets. Bat Masterson, his deputy, then appeared, shot the Texan and one of his pals dead and wounded several others. It was all a rather rough-and-ready business in which showing nerve and skill with a gun were part of the show.

The Colt Peacemaker or Frontier Model was the most popular revolver in the 1870s but a number of single- and double-action revolvers were also favoured. Many of the professional gunmen on both sides of the law owned a variety of guns. Wild Bill Hickok is said to have carried quite an assortment during his career, including an 1848 Colt Dragoon, a pair of 1851 Navy Colts plus two single-shot pistols by Henry Derringer, an English .45 Deane, Adams and Deane and, towards the end of his career, a .44 Smith and Wesson. Both Wyatt Earp and Doc Holliday used Colt Peacemakers.

Wyatt, by all accounts, was one of the coolest of the marshals, steadily firing aimed shots and making each one tell. At one time Marshal of Dodge City, he was one of the few to die of old age. The Earp brothers, Morgan, Virgil and Wyatt, were mixed up in the controversial gunfight in which all four of the McLowry gang were killed and Morgan Earp wounded. There has been much speculation as to who started the shooting and which party was the most to blame.

The single-shot percussion pistols made by Henry Derringer, a Philadelphia gunsmith, are interesting mainly because his catchy surname was later applied to a type of small pocket pistol with a relatively heavy calibre. The original pistols were rather crudely-finished short-barrelled muzzle-loaders with a back-action lock and curled 'bird's head' butt. They were much imitated and were used for several notorious crimes including the assassination of President Lincoln by John Wilkes Booth. Later cartridge models were made by Colt and a neatly-made .41 over-and-under double-barrelled Derringer was produced by Remington. These pistols were great favourites as weapons of self-defence because they could be carried unobtrusively but delivered a knock-down blow when needed.

Most double-barrelled shotguns were imported into America from such places as Birmingham and Liège, where they were produced cheaply in large numbers. However, in 1882 the Spencer repeating shotgun appeared, the magazine of which lay in a tube under the barrel, and it was operated by the back-and-forward movement of the left-hand grip, usually referred to as a pump action. And in 1887 the Winchester repeating shotgun was introduced; this was

A group of Cheyenne Indians, led by Tall Bull, attack a hand-car crew near Fossil Creek, Kansas, on 28 May 1869

Cowboys fighting off an Indian attack with Colts and Winchesters. 'An episode in the opening up of a cattle country', one of Frederic Remington's illustrations for *Ranch Life and the Hunting Trail* by Theodore Roosevelt.

operated by the well-known Winchester under-lever. It was designed by John M. Browning, the famous designer of automatic arms, who also designed a pump-action shotgun for Remington. Later he designed the well-known Browning automatic shotgun and the famous Browning over-and-under double-barrelled shotgun.

The legend of the West may be said to have started with the blood-and-thunder tales of Ned Buntline, who was inspired to write his serial 'Buffalo Bill, King of the Border Men' after a meeting with William Cody in 1869. He later persuaded his hero to take part in a dramatization of his adventures. Cody, however, soon decided to go into business on his own account and the famous *Buffalo Bill's Wild West Show* was born. The tremendous success of this show was such that it travelled over America and parts of Europe, bringing to its audiences an exciting and romanticized version of the West. This Western legend has since never ceased to be expanded in books, films and television serials, until today the bark of the six-shooter and the whine of a ricocheting Winchester bullet may be heard in many strangely incongruous parts of the world.

The needs of the frontier are no more, but the enthusiasm for using and collecting guns is widespread in America today. Nowhere in the world is there such a variety of firearms and ammunition available, and nowhere are there more guns in private hands.

The fine-quality Smith and Wesson centre-fire revolver, Model 1881. This revolver hinges open to assist loading.

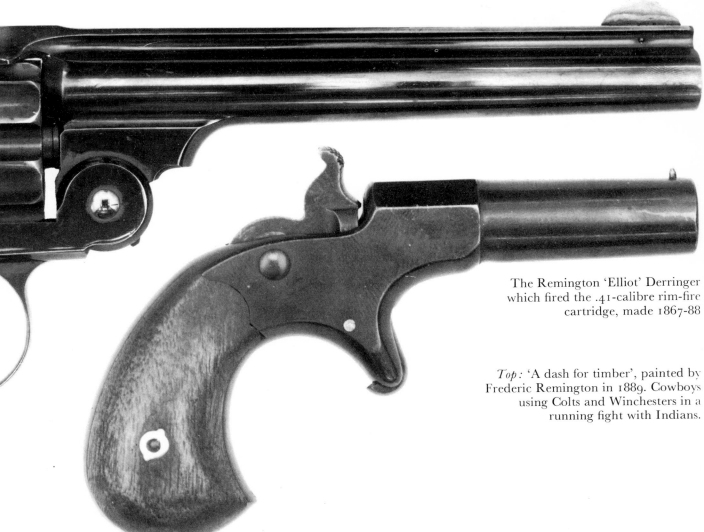

The Remington 'Elliot' Derringer
which fired the .41-calibre rim-fire
cartridge, made 1867-88

Top: 'A dash for timber', painted by
Frederic Remington in 1889. Cowboys
using Colts and Winchesters in a
running fight with Indians.

Duelling pistols

Duels in the seventeenth and first half of the eighteenth century had for the most part been fought with swords. First rapiers and later small-swords were used. Gentlemen wore small-swords as part of their normal town-dress in the latter half of the seventeenth and in the eighteenth century so they were the most convenient weapons to hand. However, duels had occasionally been fought with pistols, and any pair of pistols that was available was used, although it was mostly holster or cavalry pistols.

Probably because a skilled swordsman had such an unfair advantage over one less skilled, pistols became more popular for duelling in the mid-eighteenth century. Also there was more of an element of chance with pistols, when both could miss, perhaps deliberately, and with honour served make up the quarrel. Be the reason what it may, pistols soon ousted the sword almost entirely in Britain and America, although swords and sabres retained some popularity in Europe.

In Britain in the middle of the eighteenth century holster pistols or travelling pistols were often used, the firing taking place at an agreed signal and distance. A generally-accepted practice grew up whereby the pistols were loaded under the supervision of the seconds, then the aggrieved parties took their pistols, stood back-to-back, walked the required number of paces, turned and fired. There were several variations, including instances where one party fired first or they aimed their pistols first and then fired on the word being given. There were also some duels in which the shooting was at very close range. However it was the standard type of duel that was to cause a specialized pistol to be designed. The type of pistol needed was one that pointed quite naturally at the target

A typical pair of flintlock duelling pistols by Robert Wogdon, *c.* 1780, shown in their case with powder flask, bullet mould and cleaning rod

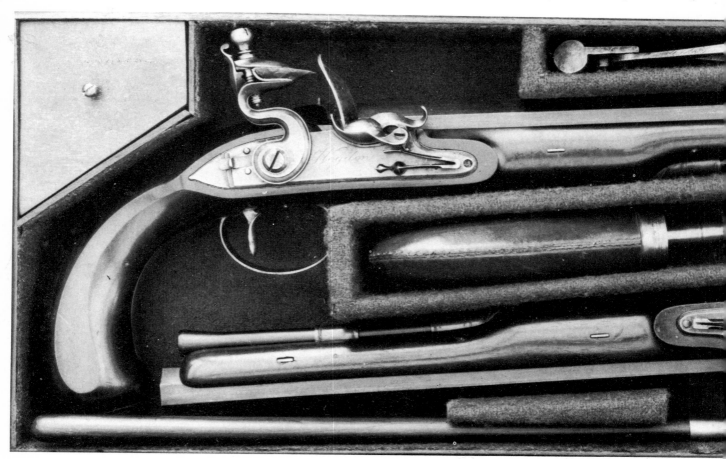

when the arm was raised and was both steady and reliable on every occasion on which it was fired.

Robert Wogdon was one of the best known of the late eighteenth-century gunmakers to specialize in pistols designed for duelling. Wogdon created a plain workmanlike pistol with an octagonal barrel about ten inches long and of 28 bore. The full stock was finished in a plain, curved, flat-sided butt which fitted the hand in such a way that the pistol came up naturally pointing at the target. The lock was improved, as in sporting guns of the period, to make it quicker and more reliable. The furniture, of lightly-engraved iron, was charcoal blued and the barrel browned so that no light reflected from shiny surfaces. The sights were also charcoal blued.

In the late eighteenth century it became usual for pairs of duelling pistols to be sold in baize-lined polished wooden cases with compartments for the pistols, powder flask, bullet mould, loading and cleaning rods, spare flints and leathers, and perhaps a turnscrew and an oil bottle.

By the early nineteenth century flintlock duelling pistols were ideally suited to their purpose. Many superb pistols were made by such gunmakers as Mortimer, Egg, Rigby, Gulley, Nock, Twigg and the Mantons. Typical of this period were pistols with heavier octagonal barrels fitted with patent cut-away breeches, half-stocked with a curved chequered butt. The locks were of the latest type with narrow 'rainproof' pans and a short sharp action to the cock. Set or hair triggers were often fitted, adjustable by means of a tiny screw, and a little steel piece called a 'detant' was added to the tumbler to ride the sear smoothly over the half-cock bent or notch. When set, the trigger fired the pistol at the slightest touch.

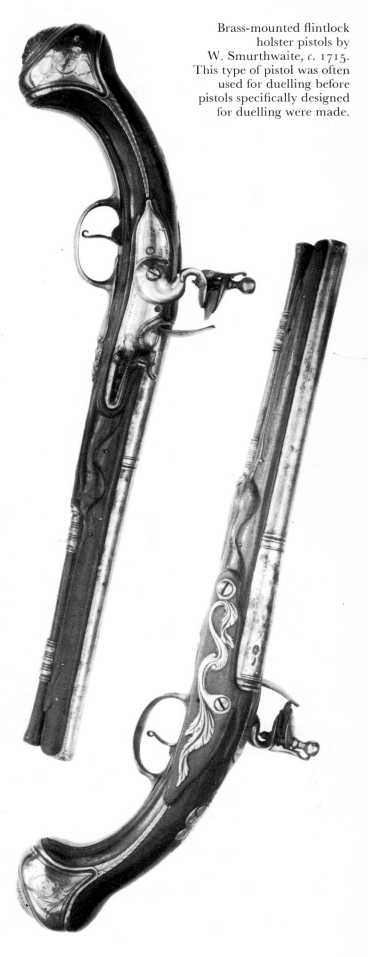

Brass-mounted flintlock holster pistols by W. Smurthwaite, c. 1715. This type of pistol was often used for duelling before pistols specifically designed for duelling were made.

A fine pair of half-stocked flintlock duelling pistols by McCormick of Dublin, c. 1795. Note the heavy octagonal barrels and the chequered butt. Here shown in their case with bullet mould, powder flask, turnscrew and cleaning rod.

Right: A superb pair of French duelling pistols signed 'Boutet, Directeur Artiste, Manufacture à Versailles', c. 1800. They are shown in their fine fitted leather-lined case with equipment including loading rods and mallets for tapping down the tight-fitting bullets into the rifled barrel.

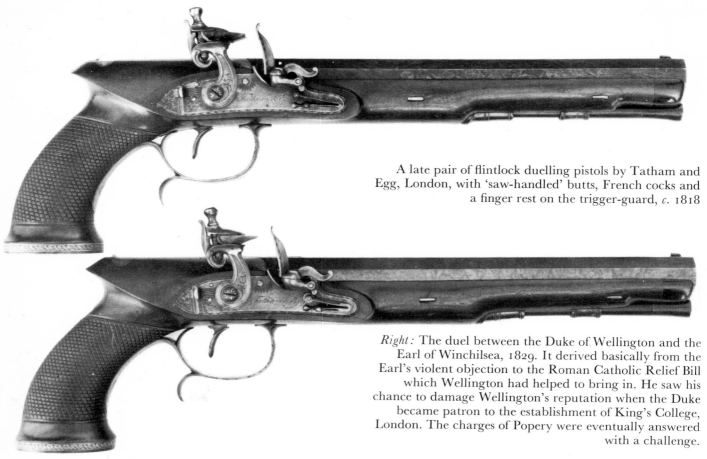

A late pair of flintlock duelling pistols by Tatham and Egg, London, with 'saw-handled' butts, French cocks and a finger rest on the trigger-guard, *c.* 1818

Right: The duel between the Duke of Wellington and the Earl of Winchilsea, 1829. It derived basically from the Earl's violent objection to the Roman Catholic Relief Bill which Wellington had helped to bring in. He saw his chance to damage Wellington's reputation when the Duke became patron to the establishment of King's College, London. The charges of Popery were eventually answered with a challenge.

Some pistols at this time were stocked with a projection to the rear top of the butt that fitted between the first finger and thumb; this was usually described as a 'saw-butt' and was a help in holding the pistol steady. This was important because there could easily be a movement in the delay between the pulling of the trigger and the ignition of the main charge. This was the reason why a heavy barrel, a good grip and a light trigger were all essential to accurate shooting. Of course, triggers that were too light could be pulled before the dueller intended, especially if he was nervous or his fingers cold.

It was customary for British duelling pistols to be smooth bored, though European ones were often rifled. However, some British pistols were rifled, but the last inch was bored smooth to hide it. Other pistols have what is known as scratch rifling, which is so fine that it would not normally be noticed.

Great care was taken with the loading of duelling pistols. The balls used were cast so as to make sure that there was no hollow part in them and then they were filed smooth where the sprue had been cut off. The exact measure of powder was put into the hollow end of the loading rod and the barrel placed muzzle down over the rod. When the pistol and rod were turned so that the muzzle faced upwards, the powder was deposited straight into the breech. This method of loading prevented the powder from straggling all the way down the bore.

The ball was then put onto a soft leather or linen patch placed centrally over the bore and carefully rammed down onto the powder. To test if the powder load was right for the bullet, the ball was fired at a steel plate. If the ball fell off, neatly spread to a circle about one inch wide, then it was about

right. If, however, the lead was spattered to pieces, the charge was too heavy, and, if the bullet failed to spread, the load was judged to be insufficient. Although most British pistols were unrifled, they were nevertheless quite accurate enough to be sure of hitting a man in the chest at 25 yards with a carefully-aimed shot.

The earlier guncases had mostly been made of oak, but, as the idea of owning a fine cased set of pistols became fashionable, so superb mahogany cases were made with a circular brass drop-handle. The trade-label inside the lid was elaborately engraved with fine lettering and scrolls and often surmounted by the Royal Arms. The fittings in the later cases tended to be more extensive and of fine quality. These cased pairs of duelling pistols obviously had something of the appeal to their contemporaries that they have to collectors today. Certain pairs of pistols were made with rich silver mounts but these were usually for presentation or prestige sets, rather than sets intended for use at dawn. While on the subject of cased pairs of pistols, it should be understood that it was also customary to case officers', travelling and even pocket pistols in a similar manner. For this reason these are sometimes mistaken for duelling pistols. The travelling and pocket pistols can easily be distinguished by their shorter barrels, but officers' pistols can look almost identical except for their larger bores; later ones often have swivel ramrods. This does not mean, however, that all these types of pistol were not occasionally pressed into service when the correct pistols were unavailable. The reason why officers' pistols looked very similar to duelling pistols was that the attention given to the design of duellers had a considerable influence

on the design of military and travelling pistols of the period.

The duels themselves were not always the romantic affairs of honour that they are sometimes supposed. Duels were often fought for the most trivial reasons. Once the challenge was made it was difficult 'honourably' to avoid a duel. Ireland was notorious for the picking of quarrels and duelling for the sake of duelling. There was certainly little sympathy or respect for the duellists in the press reports, as the following, from the *Annals of Sporting 1822*, suggests: 'Ireland. Three duels by three persons in which species of "battle" two of them "napt" it tidily is no "bul" but savouring a good deal of the "blarney". Yes; two men have been shot in cold blood and we choose to grin at their misfortunes in order to vex their seconds, and all other abettors, seeing the thing might have been settled more amicably.'

Another report is of an exchange of shots between O'Meary and M'Laughlin in Phoenix Park, Dublin. Both missed and there was a further exchange later in the week in which one of the seconds (or bottle holder as the report has it) took over as principal. This exchange failing to draw blood, the original contestants had a third exchange, in which both were wounded. The report concludes with a note: 'that those who would know what becomes of the survivors in this miscreantish affair must wait for the next Dublin Assizes.'

The duel-provoking Sir Lucius O'Trigger in *The Rivals* by Sheridan (1775) seems to have been well drawn from the tendency of some Irishmen to take up pistols for little more reason than the desire to exchange shots with someone. In the following scene Sir Lucius tries to make sure that the contestants are close enough to ensure hits.

Act V   Scene iii   *Enter Sir Lucius O'Trigger and Acres, with pistols.*

ACRES. By my valour! then, Sir Lucius, forty yards is a good distance. Odds levels and aims! – I say it is a good distance.
SIR LUCIUS. Is it for muskets or small field-pieces? Upon my conscience, Mr Acres, you must leave those things to me. – Stay now – I'll show you. – (*Measures paces along the stage.*) There now, that is a very pretty distance – a pretty gentleman's distance.
ACRES. Zounds! we might as well fight in a sentry-box! I tell you, Sir Lucius, the farther he is off, the cooler I shall take my aim.
SIR LUCIUS. Faith! then I suppose you would aim at him best of all if he was out of sight!

When in 1822 the Dukes of Bedford and Buckingham met in Kensington Gardens over a matter of alleged slander, they fired without effect at twelve paces, but as Bedford fired in the air Buckingham declared that the matter could go no further. They then made up the quarrel and parted friends. A similar sort of thing occurred in the famous duel between the Duke of Wellington and Lord Winchilsea in 1829. Lord Winchilsea did not raise his pistol arm; on seeing this the Duke fired wide.

Missing to one side or deliberately firing to one side to satisfy honour without causing injury were not without their hazards for the seconds. In a duel on Bagshot Heath in 1822 one of the seconds was shot and died shortly after; this was not an isolated incident, seconds being reported killed or wounded

by duellers on quite a number of occasions.

In America some duels were carried on in the approved European manner, as in the famous duel between General Andrew Jackson and Charles Dickinson which took place in 1806. Both were crack shots with a pistol and after firing first Dickinson was amazed to find his man still standing. Jackson then took careful aim and shot Dickinson dead. Only then was it discovered that Dickinson's shot had struck Jackson in the chest, breaking two ribs and inflicting a painful but not dangerous wound. Jackson had calmly avoided showing any sign of his injury. Apart from the formal duels, however, there were a number of unconventional ones in America, ranging from the use of revolvers to Derringers and knives.

In France pistols were quite popular for settling affairs of honour or the heart, and duelling pistols by Boutet are superb examples of the French type. These are usually set in elaborately equipped and decorated cases.

In the 1820s there was a change from the flintlock to the quicker and more reliable percussion cap. The almost-instantaneous ignition of the percussion cap was an aid to accurate shooting. Around the 1820s several London gun-makers set up shooting galleries, one of the first being Joseph Lang's in the Haymarket. Pistol shooting became quite a popular pastime, not only as practice for duelling, but also for its own sake. Some pistols were equipped with spare rifled barrels so that they could serve as duelling or target pistols.

The ability of many shooters to place all their shots in a heart-sized target at fifteen to twenty paces was a considerable deterrent to those who might otherwise have rashly got involved in a duel. This, added to the strong opposition or ridicule of public opinion and also sterner measures in the courts, caused duelling in England to diminish and finally cease by the middle of the nineteenth century.

The duelling or target pistols made by James Purdey were typical of the later style. These have a butt that curves down from the barrel at an angle of about forty-five degrees and is finished with a flat oval butt-plate. They were half stocked and there was no provision for a ramrod, a loading rod being provided. Sometimes a spur or finger rest was added to the trigger-guard. In the 1830s Purdey used a black 'ebonized' finish on some of his pistols which gave them a suitably-sombre appearance for duelling. Around the middle of the nineteenth century pistols designed specifically for target shooting were made, with rifled barrels. The rifling was normally of the multigroove type but the writer has a pair of percussion target pistols made by James Purdey in 1864 for the Maharajah of Bulrampore which have two-groove rifling of .36 calibre and small leaf-sights for 20, 40, 60, 80 and 100 yards. These are rare examples of high-velocity long-range target pistols.

In France a type of duelling and target pistol with elaborate 'Gothic' decoration was popular in the mid-nineteenth century. It was lavishly equipped and cased, also in 'Gothic' style.

With the introduction of rim-fire cartridges, the .22 saloon pistol came into use for indoor target shooting. Target shooting for its own sake is still popular and is carried on with revolvers, automatics, and specially-constructed target pistols of a wide variety of types, including some with curious hand-embracing butts.

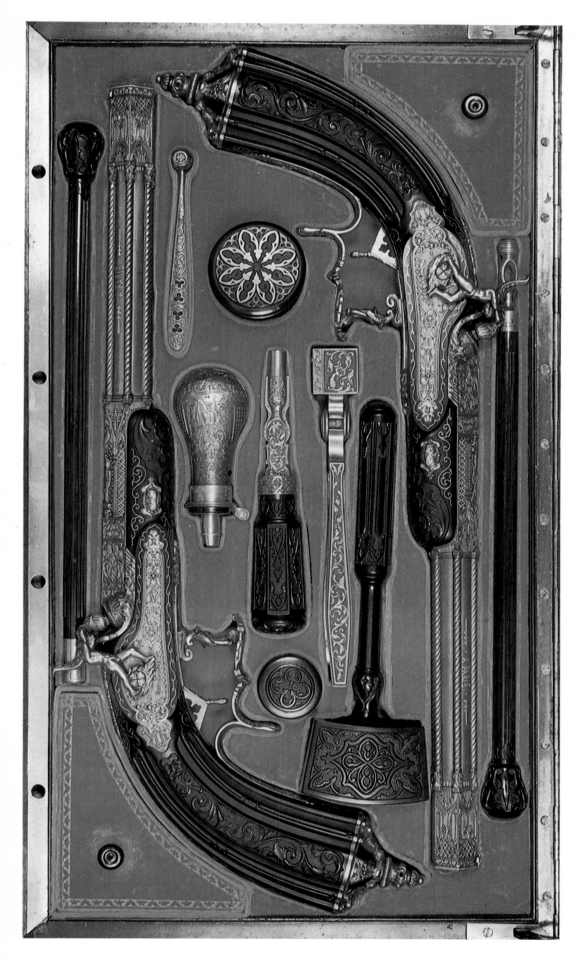

The chiselled steel and carved ebony decoration on these pistols and their equipment make them an excellent example of the most lavish Gothic style of ornament applied to duelling or target pistols. By Renette & Gastinne, Paris, *c.* 1850, they are shown in their fine velvet-lined fitted case.

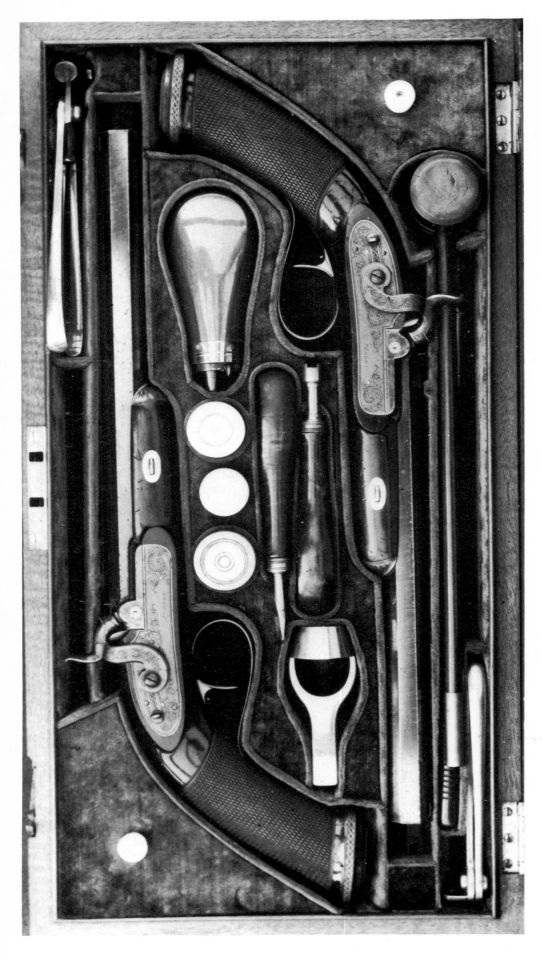

A French duel in conventional European style with the seconds on either side, *c.* 1880

A superb pair of rifled percussion-cap target pistols by James Purdey, *c.* 1835, contained in their fitted velvet-lined case with equipment including bullet mould, sprue cutter, patch cutter, nipple key and loading rods. These pistols have no ramrods and the half stocks have a black 'ebony' finish.

A finest quality target pistol, one of a pair made by James Purdey for the Maharajah of Bulrampore in 1864. It is a rare example of a two-groove rifled pistol with leaf sights for 20, 40, 60, 80, and 100 yards, and it has a set or hair trigger.

Self-protection guns

Once guns came into general use it was not long before they were employed for murder and robbery on the one hand and for protection of self and property on the other.

Authorities in sixteenth-century Europe were much concerned at the use of guns for criminal purposes, as the following ordinances suggest. Maximillian I, Emperor of the Holy Roman Empire, prohibited the use and manufacture of wheel-lock guns in 1518. The carrying of wheel-lock guns was prohibited in the city of Ferrara in Italy in 1523. Similar ordinances were passed by the authorities of other cities who were concerned at the numbers of murders and assassinations carried out, particularly with wheel-lock pistols.

In England an ordinance of Henry VIII in 1542 drew attention to the criminal use of firearms:
'evil disposed persons . . . have wilfully and shamefully commytted, perpetrated and done diverse detestable and shamefull murthers, roberies, felonyes, ryotts and routes with crosbowes, lyttle short hand guns and lyttle hagbutts, to the great perill and contynuall fear and danger of the Kings most lovinge subjects . . . nowe of late the saide eville disposed persons have used and yet doe daylie use to ride and go in the Kings highe wayes and elsewhere, having with them crosbowes and little handguns ready furnished with quarrel gunpowder, fyer and touche, to the great perill and feare of the Kings most loving subjects.'

The short matchlock guns referred to above were obviously a serious nuisance in the hands of highway robbers and other criminals, but not quite such a menace as the small all-metal wheel-lock pistols in use in parts of Europe. These pistols could be hidden about the person and then used for robbery or murder at a moment's notice. Gentlemen travelling on horseback or in a coach would do so with an armed escort carrying wheel-lock pistols in their saddle holsters and petronels or other short wheel-lock guns. No doubt small wheel-lock pistols were carried, together with sword and dagger, as a defence against footpads and robbery at night.

A fine-quality pair of seventeenth-century brass-barrelled blunderbusses with brass furniture

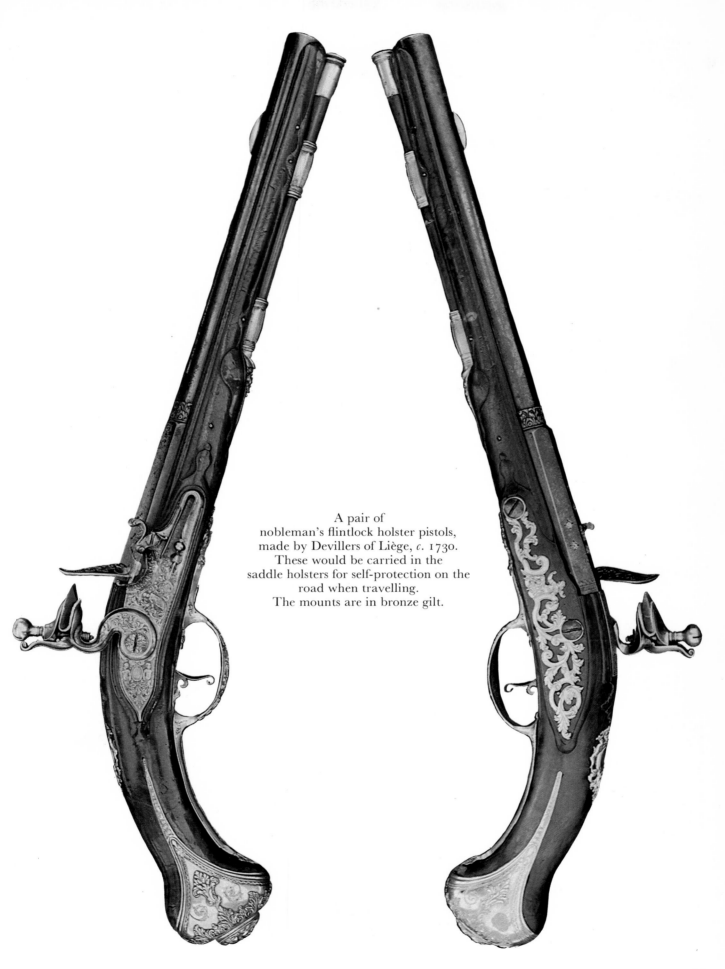

A pair of
nobleman's flintlock holster pistols,
made by Devillers of Liège, *c.* 1730.
These would be carried in the
saddle holsters for self-protection on the
road when travelling.
The mounts are in bronze gilt.

In England, in the seventeenth century, the mounted highwayman armed with pistols became a familiar figure. One, John Clavel, having been captured and sentenced to death, was reprieved by Charles I in 1626 and in consequence wrote in verse the 'Recantation of an Ill-led Life'.

After the English Civil War some Royalist soldiers took to the road as a means of making a living. They were good horsemen, well mounted, armed with a brace of flintlock holster pistols, and dressed like gentlemen, and they became the archetype for the romanticized 'gentlemen of the road' immortalized in the character of Captain Macheath in John Gay's *The Beggar's Opera*.

Captain Howard was a Royalist officer turned highwayman who robbed both the Earl of Essex and the Earl of Pembroke and is said to have robbed Cromwell himself at an inn in Chester. He was finally caught at Blackheath when

A small all-steel wheel-lock pistol or dag from Saxony, such as was carried for self-protection, robbery or murder, *c.* 1590

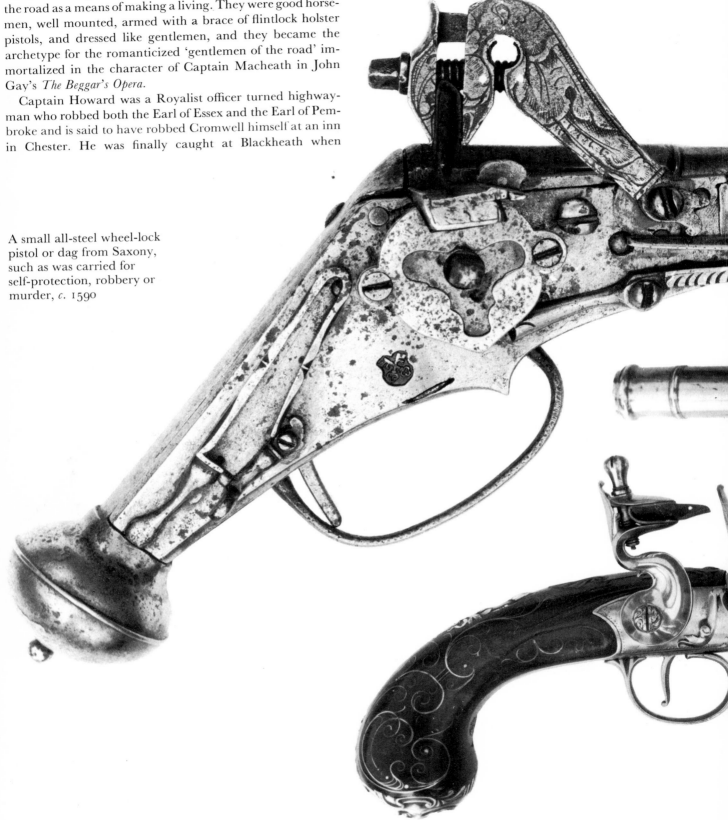

attempting to attack six officers and was hanged in 1652. Captain Hind was another officer who fought in the Civil War and attained a reputation for daring and gallantry on the highway; he was condemned and hanged for treason in 1652. Claude Duval was a Frenchman who came to England as a servant to one of the exiles returning with Charles II. He soon took to the road and was noted for his dalliance with the fair sex, in particular the episode when he danced on the heath with a lady from a coach which he and his associates had held up.

In spite of the popular legend naming Dick Turpin, Nicks was probably the man who rode from London to York in fifteen hours and he is said to have been pardoned by Charles II in return for relating how he had accomplished the feat. Charles apparently named him 'Swift' Nicks. Dick Turpin was an inferior type of highwayman who started as a butcher

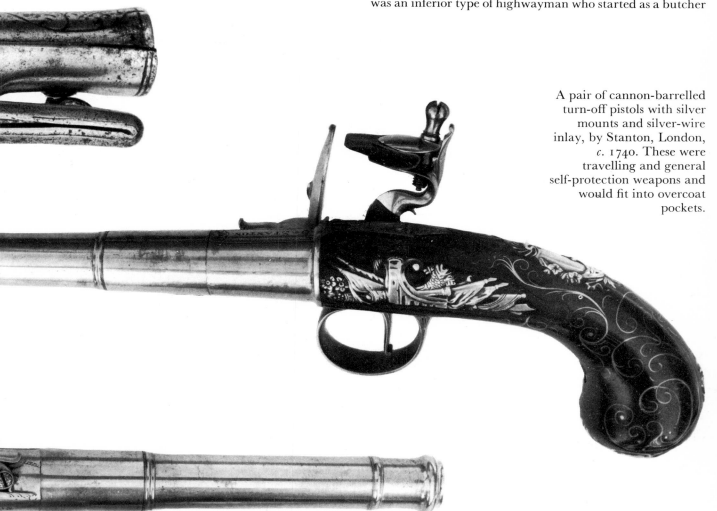

A pair of cannon-barrelled turn-off pistols with silver mounts and silver-wire inlay, by Stanton, London, c. 1740. These were travelling and general self-protection weapons and would fit into overcoat pockets.

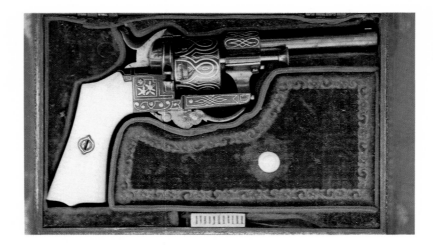

A pin-fire pocket
revolver in its velvet
case, made in Liège,
c. 1860

A fine pair of
flintlock, turn-off
pocket pistols, the
butts richly inlaid
with silver, made by
Mortimer of
St James's, London,
c. 1815. They are
shown in their
velvet-lined
mahogany case with
equipment including
the ring lever for
turning off the short
barrels for loading,
the powder flask, the
turnscrew and the
bullet mould.

Far right: 'John
Cottington alias
Mul-Sack, robbing
the Oxford waggon
wherein he found four
thousand pounds in
money', an illustration
from Captain
Alexander Smith's
history of
highwaymen,
footpads, shoplifts and
cheats of both sexes.
The money had been
levied by Cromwell's
Rump Parliament and
was being taken in
convoy to Oxford and
Gloucester to pay the
soldiers there.
Cottington is supposed
to have got his alias
Mul-Sack because of
his particular fondness
for this beverage.

A fine silver-
mounted pair of
pocket pistols of the
boxlock, turn-off
type by James
Wilkinson and Son,
London, *c.* 1815

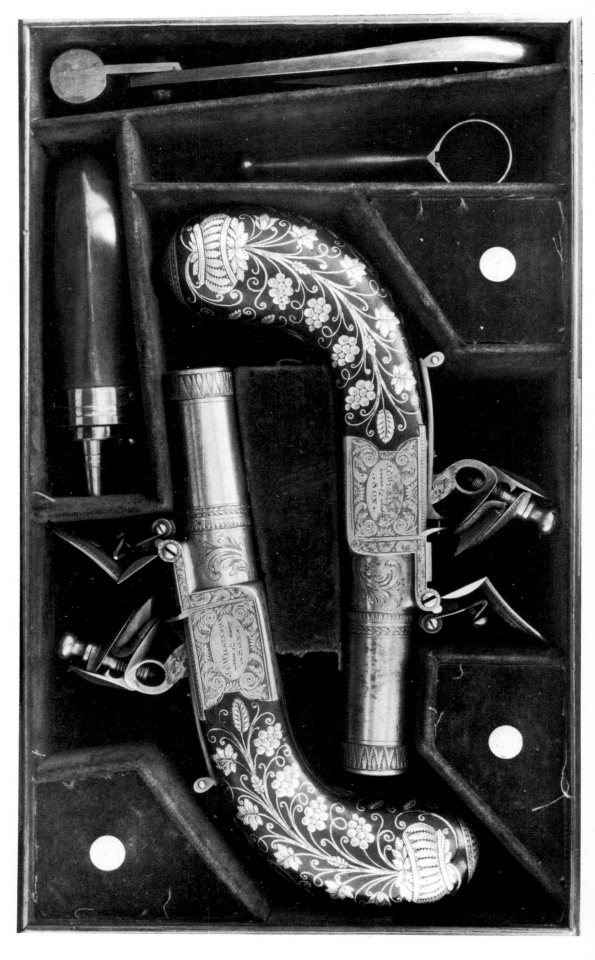

and cattle thief, did some highway robberies with Tom King and was hanged for horse-stealing in 1739.

When robbery on the highway became commonplace, special pistols, called 'coach' or 'travelling' pistols, were developed. Such pistols were shorter than holster pistols, being of a suitable size to put in an overcoat pocket. One of the most popular types of self-protection pistol during most of the eighteenth century was the cannon-barrelled turn-off pistol with a silver mask butt plate. These graceful sidelock pistols had derived from the military turn-off pistols used in the Civil War. In the first part of the century they had sidelocks with pierced silver side plates on the other side. A few small pocket pistols of this type were also made, with a short barrel and a rounded wooden butt.

After the middle of the eighteenth century these turn-off pistols are mostly fitted with a central boxlock. Short boxlock turn-off pocket pistols were made in large numbers. These were also made with double barrels arranged in the over-and-under manner, the priming and touch-hole for the lower barrel being brought into position by the turning of a tap on the side of the pan. A few pistols with more than two barrels were made, including the 'duck's foot' or mob pistols in which four barrels were arranged like opened fingers. These fired together from a central boxlock, giving a wide arc of fire; they were most useful as close-range weapons in keeping a mob at bay.

Towards the end of the eighteenth century it became common for small flick-out bayonets to be fitted under the barrels of boxlock pocket pistols. Similar types of turn-off pocket pistols continued to be popular through the percussion era, the nineteenth-century ones mostly having flat-sided butts for fitting snugly into pockets.

Of all the guns associated with the protection of self and property, the blunderbuss has a special place. This relatively short-barrelled gun with a large bell mouth first appeared in Europe in the early seventeenth century and in England in the middle of that century. The blunderbuss was designed for shooting a quantity of small shot, such as buck shot or swan shot, at relatively close range. Though the bell mouth suggested that the shot would spread very widely, this was not so. In fact the shot spread no more than from a cylinder barrel of the same length. However, the great bell mouth was most intimidating: those at whom it was aimed were convinced that there was no escaping the dreadful blast.

Round the muzzle of some blunderbusses is engraved the warning legend: 'Happy is he that escapeth me'. As protection weapons they were carried by the guards of coaches. For the landlords of inns and in many households the blunderbuss also became the standard deterrent against robbery. The traditional place for keeping the blunderbuss was on the chimney-breast over the fireplace or range. This was not a matter of its looking well in this position, though it did indeed do so. It was necessary for the blunderbuss to be kept loaded and primed if it was to be ready for immediate use, so the chimney-breast was an ideal warm dry place to keep both the priming and main charge perfectly dry.

The brass barrel of the blunderbuss possibly derived from the fact that the weapon was originally used on board ships, where it was a suitable close-range weapon for confined space or for repelling boarders. A barrel that did not rust was also of advantage to coach guards. Towards the end of the eighteenth century, the fitting of spring-out bayonets to blunderbusses became general. Mostly these were fitted to the top of the barrel and were released by a catch behind the top of the breech. Many fine blunderbusses were made by the Birmingham firm of Ketland and some of the most superb late ones by the renowned Henry Nock. Brass-barrelled blunderbuss pistols were made in various sizes in the eighteenth and nineteenth centuries, and some of these were also fitted with bayonets.

In the late eighteenth and first half of the nineteenth century, travelling or coach pistols followed the same general lines as did duelling pistols, except that the barrels were much shorter and the general scale of the pistols smaller. The bore, however, was as large or larger than that of a duelling pistol.

Following the sidelock flint and percussion travelling pistols came the multi-barrelled pepperbox. Revolving pistols and pepperboxes had been tried out in the flintlock era, particularly in the early nineteenth century. However, it was the introduction of the percussion copper cap which was to make these pistols a practical proposition and lead to their widespread use. Large numbers of double-action pepperboxes were manufactured in Birmingham and Liège between about 1830 and 1860. The number of barrels averaged about five or six but some have many more. These pistols could be drawn and fired quickly as the pull of the trigger both turned the barrels and also cocked and released the hammer. For self-protection at close range they were ideal, not least for the effect that looking down some six or so barrels had on robbers, mobs, mutineers and such like miscreants.

The main drawbacks to pepperboxes were that they could not be accurately aimed and their multiple barrels made them heavy and cumbersome to carry. After a number of transitional designs, very well-made percussion revolvers were brought out in the mid-nineteenth century by Adams, Tranter, Webley and others. Also, of course, Colt appeared at the 1851 Exhibition with his revolvers.

The revolver soon began to replace other types of gun as the most useful and conveniently-carried self-protection weapon. When centre-fire cartridges came in, percussion revolvers were either converted or replaced by cartridge models. In Belgium large numbers of cheap pin-fire revolvers and pepperboxes were made. Small single- and double-barrelled cartridge pistols were brought out for carrying in a waistcoat pocket.

Highway robbery had declined in England by the mid-eighteenth century, but it became very widespread in nineteenth-century Australia. Bushrangers, as highwaymen were called in Australia, became something of a menace to travellers and settlers in the 1820s. John or Jack Donahue and his associates engaged in a number of hold-ups, escapes from prison and fights with the mounted police. He was eventually shot dead in 1830 by one of the mounted police following up the robbery of two carts by Donahue, Walmsley and Webber. By some perverse streak in human nature, Donahue became a folk hero in Australia, immortalized in the ballad 'Bold Jack Donahue'. Jack Duggan is another, later example of a bushranger immortalized in a folk ballad, 'The Wild Colonial Boy'. According to the words of the song he started bushranging in 1861 and the crime for which he was particularly

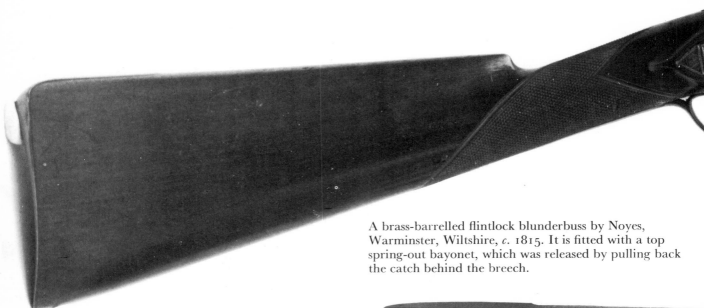

A brass-barrelled flintlock blunderbuss by Noyes, Warminster, Wiltshire, c. 1815. It is fitted with a top spring-out bayonet, which was released by pulling back the catch behind the breech.

A duck's foot, mob or mutiny pistol with flintlock, brass frame and brass barrels. All four barrels fire together. Made by Goodwin, London, c. 1800, it is fitted with a belt hook.

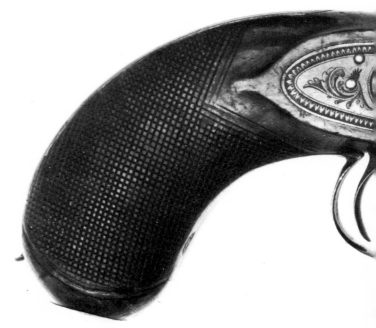

noted was the holding up of the Beechwood mailcoach and the robbing of Judge Macavoy. Jack Duggan was eventually wounded and captured by troopers Kelly, Davis and Fitzroy when he tried to shoot it out using a revolver.

In 1861 the troopers trying to arrest the bushranger Frank Gardiner had a lucky escape. One was hit in the hand, cheek and hip, and the other in the forehead, but fortunately Gardiner was using an 1836 Paterson Colt of .31 calibre which had a low striking energy. Gardiner subsequently took to using a .44-calibre Colt. He was later captured, imprisoned and then deported on release.

There was a great increase in bushranging and crime when in 1851 the Australian gold rush started. Of the later bush-rangers the most notorious were the Kellys. Armed with a small arsenal of rifles and revolvers, they robbed and murdered widely for a number of years. In 1880 came the fight with the police in which the Kellys appeared to be immune to bullets. Eventually an extraordinary figure came out of the inn where the Kelly gang were surrounded. The bulky shape was wearing a long dust-coat and appeared to have an iron can for a head. The figure advanced, firing at the police with a revolver; the shots from the police had no effect until at last the mystery gunman was shot in the knees, fell and was soon overpowered. It was Ned Kelly, wearing armour a quarter of an inch thick made from ploughshares as protection for his head and body; this had been dented in a number of places but had not been penetrated. Kelly was hanged in Melbourne Gaol in 1880.

The double-barrelled shotgun firing cartridges loaded with buckshot fulfilled much the same function of protection in lonely places as the blunderbuss had in earlier times. In America shotguns were often used for law enforcement and the guards 'rode shotgun' on the Wells-Fargo stage coaches.

Where there is a need in these days for self-protection weapons the revolver has been largely superseded by neat, compact and powerful automatic pistols.

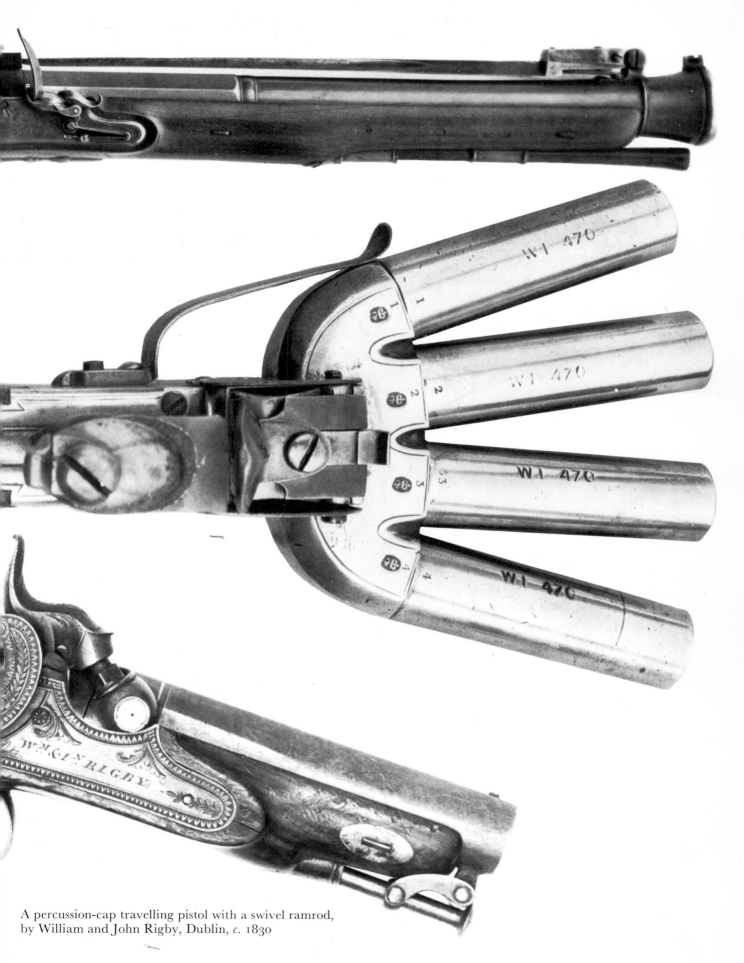

A percussion-cap travelling pistol with a swivel ramrod,
by William and John Rigby, Dublin, *c.* 1830

A fine-quality percussion
cap pepperbox by Joseph
Lang, London, c. 1845,
shown in its case with
equipment

Far right: Ned Kelly
wearing his armour made
from ploughshares attempts
to shoot it out with the
troopers, Australia, 1880

Far right below: 'Bailed up',
a painting by Tom Roberts.
Bushrangers hold up a stage
coach in New South Wales,
Australia, c. 1870

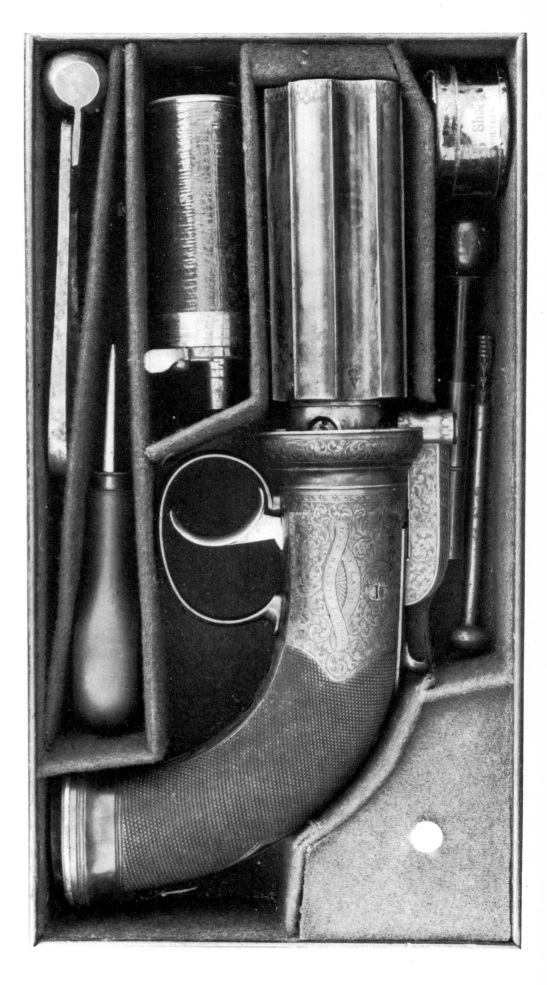

Agents for the Federal Bureau of Investigation shooting it
out with gangsters during Prohibition (1919–33). One is
using a Thompson submachine gun.

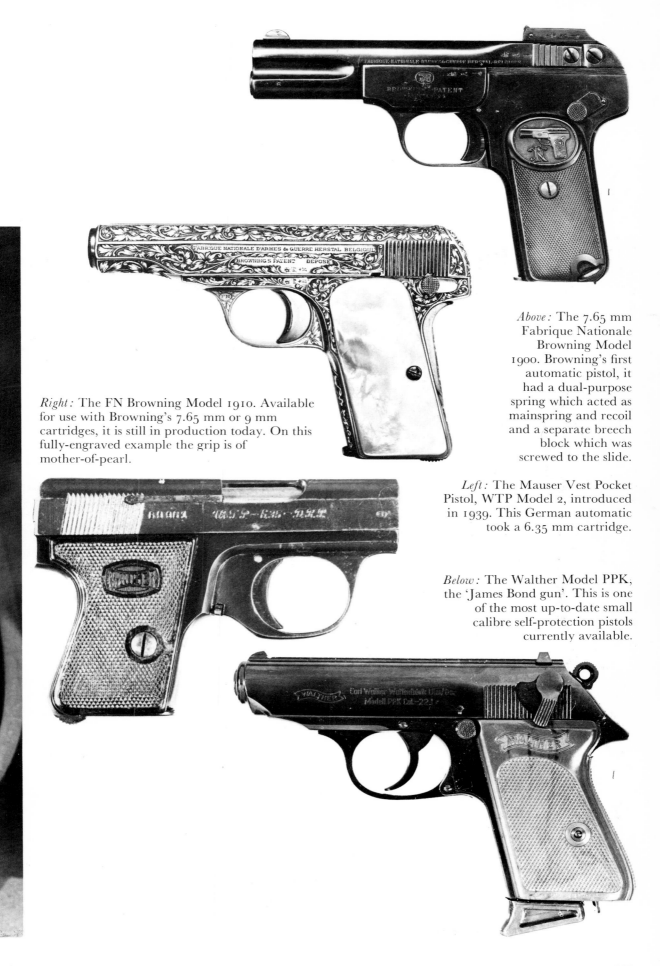

Above: The 7.65 mm Fabrique Nationale Browning Model 1900. Browning's first automatic pistol, it had a dual-purpose spring which acted as mainspring and recoil and a separate breech block which was screwed to the slide.

Right: The FN Browning Model 1910. Available for use with Browning's 7.65 mm or 9 mm cartridges, it is still in production today. On this fully-engraved example the grip is of mother-of-pearl.

Left: The Mauser Vest Pocket Pistol, WTP Model 2, introduced in 1939. This German automatic took a 6.35 mm cartridge.

Below: The Walther Model PPK, the 'James Bond gun'. This is one of the most up-to-date small calibre self-protection pistols currently available.

The decoration of guns

From the time that weapons were first made, there has been in every part of the world an appreciation of those that were particularly well made and reliable. Weapons that are functionally ideal for their purpose have a balance and perfection of form and shape in much the same way that the fastest birds, beasts and fishes are supremely graceful in their chosen elements.

In addition to the natural beauty of form and proportion in fine weapons intended for use, there have always been some weapons that have been enriched with decoration. In the first instance, decoration was added which in no way impaired their function, but, as time went on, certain weapons were so richly decorated for chieftains, princes and kings that they were reserved primarily for ceremonial purposes.

So it was with guns. In the first instance they were purely functional, but later they were finely finished and enriched with decoration until they became as much works of art as weapons. A further stage was reached in which both the nobility and the wealthy commissioned the making of guns that were primarily works of art, being rarely, if ever, fired.

Where the carving of the stock of a gun made it uncomfortable to handle, or the decoration was easily damaged, or the deep carving of the lock made it weak or difficult to clean, then the functional fitness of the gun was impaired. Equally, ornament was usually best when a balance was preserved between enriched and plain or natural surfaces. Where the stock was of a beautifully grained and figured piece of wood, this was best left free from too much carving or silver-wire inlay. It then provided a better compliment to the silver or steel furniture. A fine stub-twist or Damascus barrel likewise was seen to its best advantage either plain or with any carving or gold inlay concentrated in one or two places.

The sixteenth and first half of the seventeenth century was a period particularly noted for the use of inlay and veneers on gun stocks. Stagshorn was the most popular inlay but bone, ivory, horn and mother-of-pearl were also used. Veneers were of such woods as burr walnut and ebony and also of such rich materials as tortoiseshell, ivory or mother-of-pearl.

The inlays were cut, pierced and engraved in the most intricate and varied of designs, ranging from classical to

A pair of German wheel-lock pistols with blued and silver damascened barrels and ebony stocks profusely inlaid with engraved stagshorn depicting biblical and mythological subjects, *c.* 1565

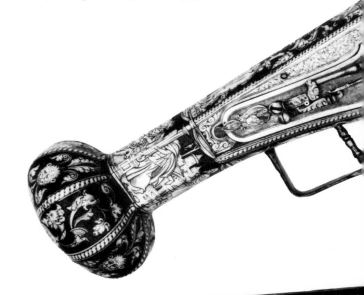

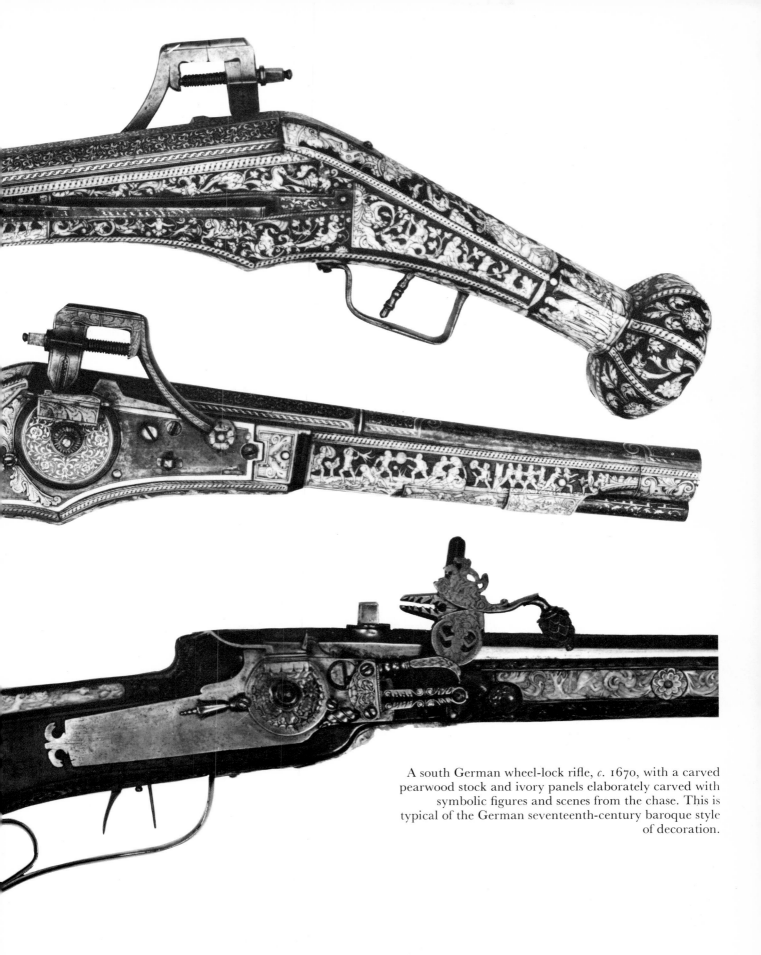

A south German wheel-lock rifle, *c.* 1670, with a carved pearwood stock and ivory panels elaborately carved with symbolic figures and scenes from the chase. This is typical of the German seventeenth-century baroque style of decoration.

Left: A detail of the lock of a Brescian wheel-lock pistol made about 1640. The arm of the cock is chiselled with acanthus-leaf ornament and its spring terminates in the head and shoulders of a woman. The ring-shaped bearing plate to the wheel has a bird's head at one end and a female figure at the other. The lock plate is bordered with engraved foliage, the rear end bearing a double-headed eagle. The stock is inlaid with typical Brescian pierced work in iron.

A detail of the finely chiselled lock on a Brescian pistol, Italian, *c.* 1670. The surface is covered with interlacing foliage and in the centre is the double eagle of Austria. The flat-sided cock is similarly decorated.

hunting and military subjects. The main groups of figures, decorative plaques, monsters or trophies of arms were often surrounded or filled in with delicate scrolls and tendrils. Though this type of decoration was widespread in Europe, the Germans were particularly noted for their exceptionally skilful work.

The engraved inlay of the stocks was complemented by the chiselling, etching and engraving of the locks. A great variety of subjects was used on the locks but the jaws that held the iron pyrites in a wheel-lock were often carved in the form of a monster's head, a decoration to which the form of the dog-head naturally lent itself. Particularly famous were the chisellers and gilders of Bavaria, who, in addition to their finely-chiselled designs, matted in and mercury gilded the ground, achieving a richly-contrasting effect. The mercury and gold powder were mixed in an amalgam and painted onto the surface to be gilt. The metal was heated to drive off the mercury in the form of a vapour, leaving the gold, which was then burnished.

In the sixteenth century, general designs for the decoration of metal objects were produced by the engravers of Nuremberg and Augsburg. These were adapted for the decoration of guns and were used in many parts of Europe for this purpose. However, by the seventeenth century pattern books of designs specifically for guns were published by engravers in the more important centres such as Paris, Nuremberg and Munich. Because of the widespread use of these designs and also because gunmakers sometimes worked away from their native towns or countries, similar designs may be found on weapons made far from the original centres of the style of decoration.

Apart from the more cosmopolitan styles of decoration, there were centres such as Brescia in Italy where distinct local styles of ornament continued unaffected by outside influences. Brescia was notable for the use of delicate pierced-steel panels let into the stock. This style of ornament reached a peak of fineness in the seventeenth century. Certainly these areas of steel lacework contrast well with the natural figure of the gracefully-shaped walnut stocks. Brescia was also famous for the making of fine barrels, particularly by the renowned Cominazzo family, the name Lazarino Cominazzo on the barrels being used as something of a family trademark. The Cominazzo family also made complete weapons with finely-chiselled locks and iron-lacework inlay set into the stocks.

Around the middle of the seventeenth century the carving of stocks tended to replace the traditional engraved-inlay work in Germany. Guns were elaborately carved with such ornament as, for example, foliated scrollwork combined with hunters and animals of the chase. By the end of the seventeenth century most gun stocks were to some extent carved, especially the area around the barrel tang to the rear of the breech and around the mounts. Late seventeenth- and eighteenth-century gun-decoration was noted for its use of well-figured

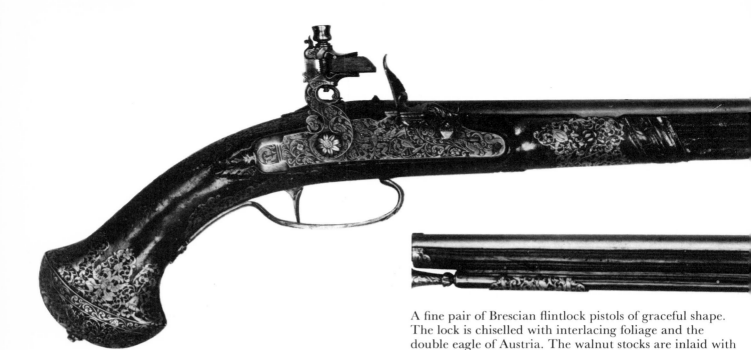

A fine pair of Brescian flintlock pistols of graceful shape. The lock is chiselled with interlacing foliage and the double eagle of Austria. The walnut stocks are inlaid with the lace-like pierced steelwork typical of Brescian ornament. The barrel is inscribed with the name of the famous Italian gunmaker Lazarino Cominazzo, *c.* 1670.

Two Parisian designs for gun decoration: *(left)* from *Plusiers Models . . .* by the gunsmiths Thuraine and le Hollandois, *c.* 1660, and *(right)* from a pattern by the engraver De Lacollombe, *c.* 1700

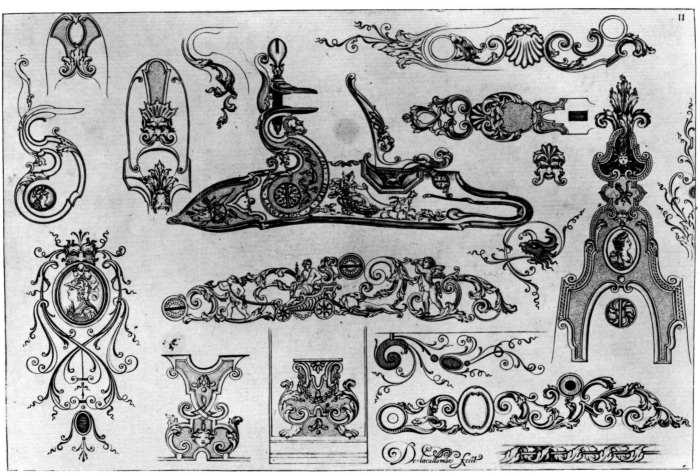

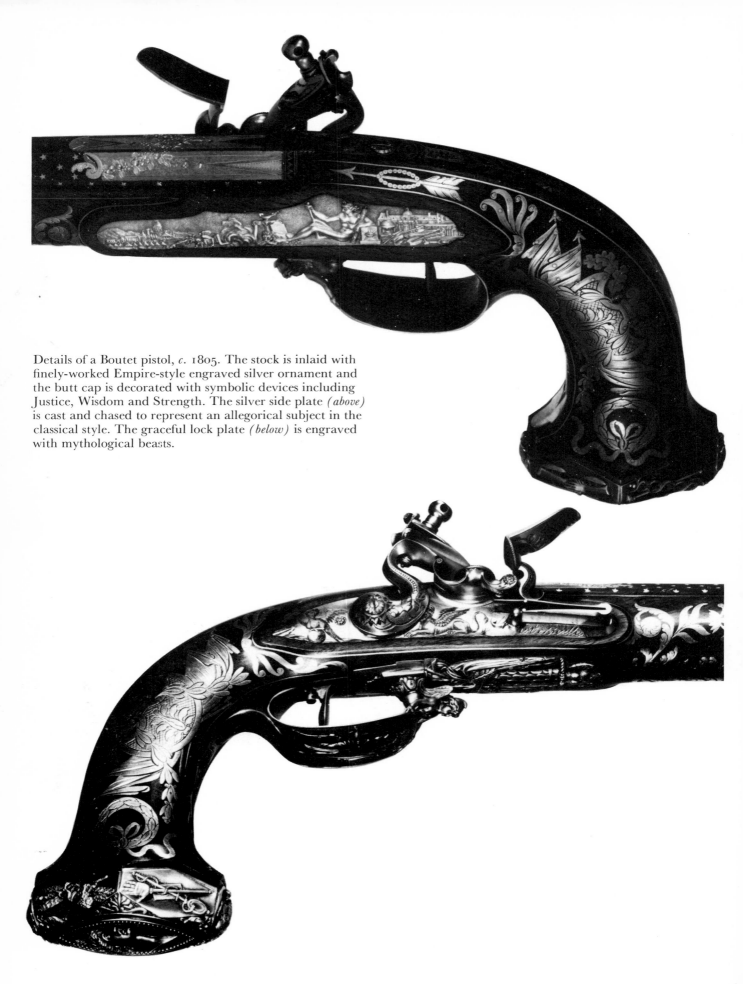

Details of a Boutet pistol, *c.* 1805. The stock is inlaid with finely-worked Empire-style engraved silver ornament and the butt cap is decorated with symbolic devices including Justice, Wisdom and Strength. The silver side plate *(above)* is cast and chased to represent an allegorical subject in the classical style. The graceful lock plate *(below)* is engraved with mythological beasts.

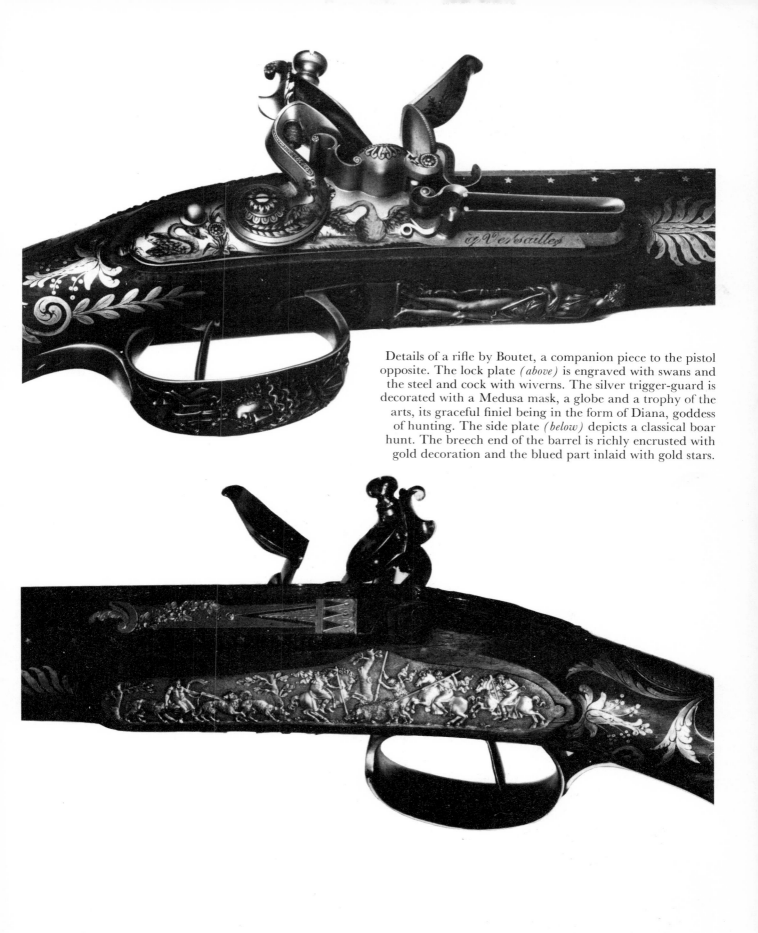

Details of a rifle by Boutet, a companion piece to the pistol opposite. The lock plate *(above)* is engraved with swans and the steel and cock with wiverns. The silver trigger-guard is decorated with a Medusa mask, a globe and a trophy of the arts, its graceful finiel being in the form of Diana, goddess of hunting. The side plate *(below)* depicts a classical boar hunt. The breech end of the barrel is richly encrusted with gold decoration and the blued part inlaid with gold stars.

Left: One of a pair of French holster pistols by 'Les La Roche aux Galleries du Louvre', *c.* 1750. The walnut stocks are carved with scrollwork and inlaid with gold wire. The lock and steel mounts are finely chiselled and the barrels are blued and encrusted with gold.

Right: A pair of gold-mounted Highland pistols presented by George III to Sir Henry Clinton. The barrels are blued, decorated with gold inlay and bear enamel portraits and plaques. They were made by Murdoch of Douane, Scotland, *c.* 1760.

Below: An English silver mounted sporting gun made by Delaney of London, *c.* 1735. The lock is plain but graceful, and the walnut stock is inlaid with silver-wire designs.

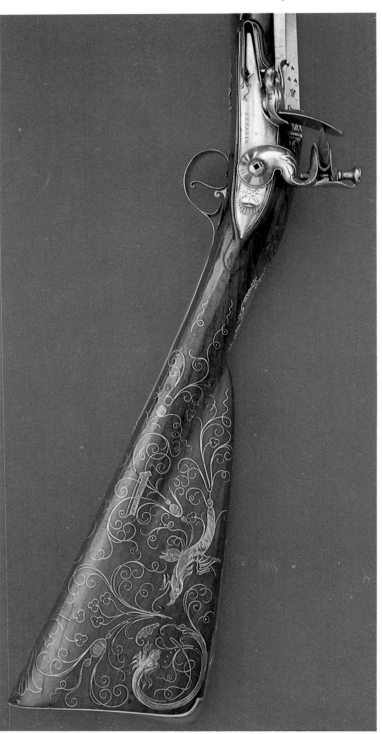

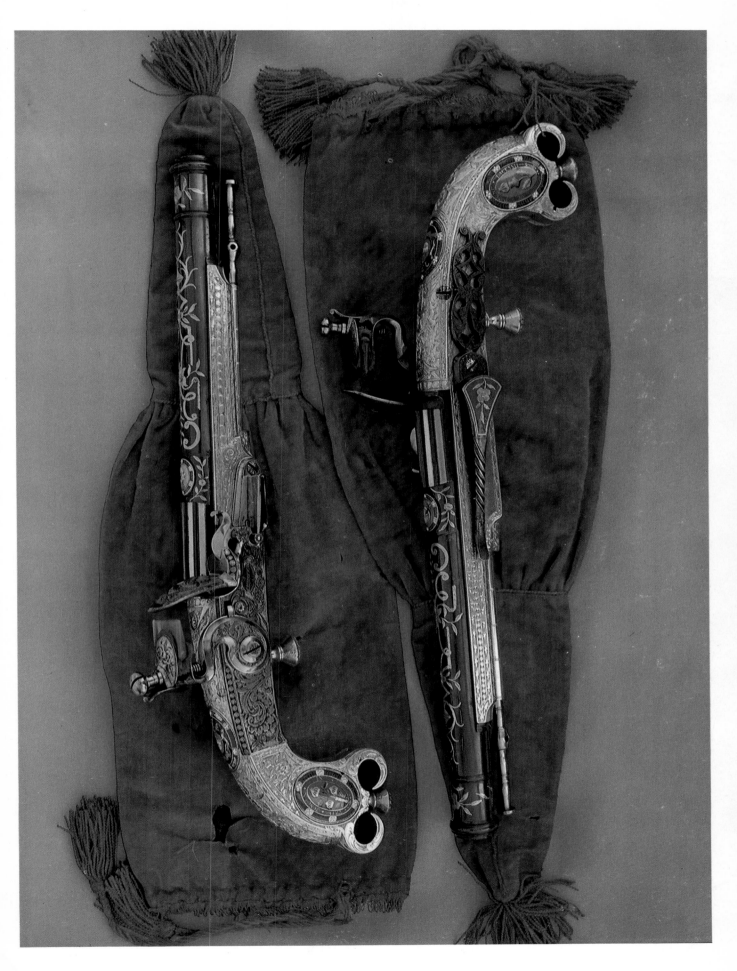

stocks, made particularly of maple and walnut, which were carved to a greater or lesser extent. The natural beauty of the wood grain was set against the richly cast and chased silver or bronze gilt furniture. The stocks were often further enriched with delicate inlays of silver wire.

The mounts of silver or bronze gilt were much easier and quicker to work than iron, which had to be wrought and painstakingly chiselled. Soft metal mounts could be cast and relatively quickly chased up to a fine finish. Particularly rich effects were used on heel plates, escutcheon plates, triggerguards and side plates. Of all the mounts, on both pistols and guns, the side plate, whose function was to retain the screws that secured the lock plate, lent itself to the most varied and elaborate treatment.

During the reigns of Louis XIII and XIV, the art of gunmaking was encouraged and as a result Paris became a major influence on the gun centres of Europe. The French type of flintlock was widely adopted, as was the Parisian fashion for rounded lock plates in the latter part of the seventeenth century. There was at the same time a change from the chiselling of designs on locks to light engraving. During the reign of Louis XIV ornament, in the form of grotesque monsters, serpents combined with foliage and hunting scenes, tended to give way to subjects drawn from classical mythology. Diana was a great favourite since the subject enabled both hunting scenes and the female form to be incorporated into the design. The legend of Leda and the swan was also widely used. Very rich effects were obtained on barrels by means of gold inlay against a fire-blued ground and sometimes areas of chiselled bright steel were contrasted against a matted gold ground.

These Parisian designs were widely known in the other gunmaking centres of Europe through the medium of pattern books of engravings and were interpreted with national variations. In England the tendency was to restrain ornament to such as would enrich without impairing the function of the gun, but some exceptional elaborately-decorated pieces were made, mostly for presentation purposes. The silver-wire and inlay work became fine and elaborate towards the middle of the eighteenth century and included such subjects as a fox hunt and scenes in the currently-fashionable Chinese style. Stocks were generally less carved in England than in Europe; a shell design or some foliage around the barrel tang was the usual extent of it.

In Germany, when they reluctantly replaced the wheellock by the French type of flintlock in the eighteenth century, they also adopted the use of richly cast and chased mounts, mostly favouring bronze gilt. In Bavaria both the mounts and the carving of the stock reflected the lively and elaborate baroque style of ornament.

Fine-quality work, generally in the Parisian style, was produced at Liège in the seventeenth and eighteenth centuries. Traditional Italian and Spanish styles of ornament were to some extent influenced in the eighteenth century by Paris, as also was the production of fine arms in Russia's Tula armoury.

Perhaps the greatest of those who excelled in artistic gunmaking was Nicolas-Noel Boutet, for in his guns, rifles and pistols he superbly combined the richest of ornament with an overall gracefulness and excellence of proportion.

Boutet was born in 1761, married the daughter of Louis

An extraordinary .44 Smith and Wesson presentation revolver decorated by Tiffany & Company in the art nouveau manner. The frame is clad in silver which extends down the butt decorated with repoussé scrolls. The bulbous ivory butt is carved with interlaced foliage and finished with a silver finiel. It was presented by Smith and Wesson to Walter Winans in 1893.

XVI's gunmaker and later succeeded to that office himself. After the Revolution, he was in 1792 appointed technical director of the newly-established State arms factory, the Manufacture de Versailles. Though mostly concerned with the supply of military weapons, there was a workshop specializing in the production of fine weapons mainly for presentation purposes. The artistic side was expanded in 1800 and Boutet took his son Pierre-Nicolas into partnership in 1804. In the years between 1800 and 1815 much of his finest work was produced, most of it being ordered for presentation purposes by the Emperor Napoleon. In 1815, after Napoleon's defeat at Waterloo, the Prussians took all that they could move from the Manufacture de Versailles. Boutet carried on privately at 87 Rue de Richelieu, taking up his pre-revolutionary appointment to the King; he died in 1833.

Boutet was responsible for a style of gunmaking which was both technically and artistically excellent, giving to the firearms he designed a shape and ornament which superbly interpreted the spirit of the Empire. The walnut stocks were neatly carved and shaped to leave plain areas to receive the engraved silver or gold inlay. The furniture was usually crisply cast and chased with motifs derived from Greek, Roman or Egyptian sources. The barrels were richly decorated in gold on a fire-blued ground, the plain areas often being covered with an overall pattern of small gold stars set at regular intervals. The graceful locks were chiselled and partly encrusted with gold. In short, the whole effect was a perfectly-balanced harmony of shape, proportion, colour and detail.

Boutet not only produced pairs of pistols superbly cased and fitted, he also produced garnitures of firearms, consisting of such combinations as a rifle and holster pistols ornamented *en suite* and set into a magnificent case lined and partitioned in velvet and fitted with all their equipment.

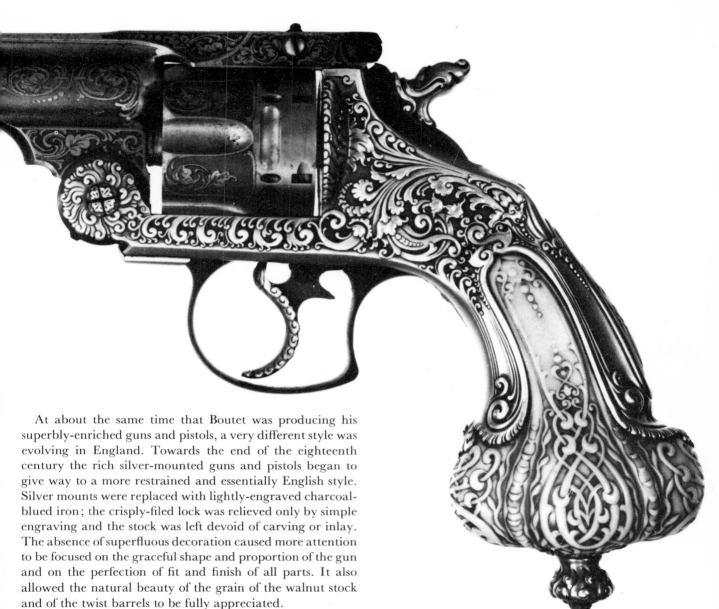

At about the same time that Boutet was producing his
superbly-enriched guns and pistols, a very different style was
evolving in England. Towards the end of the eighteenth
century the rich silver-mounted guns and pistols began to
give way to a more restrained and essentially English style.
Silver mounts were replaced with lightly-engraved charcoal-
blued iron; the crisply-filed lock was relieved only by simple
engraving and the stock was left devoid of carving or inlay.
The absence of superfluous decoration caused more attention
to be focused on the graceful shape and proportion of the gun
and on the perfection of fit and finish of all parts. It also
allowed the natural beauty of the grain of the walnut stock
and of the twist barrels to be fully appreciated.

For presentation and other purposes, finely-enriched
weapons were made with superbly cast and chased silver
mounts and barrels inlaid with gold. However the ornament
was rarely as profuse as in Europe, some areas of barrel or
stock being left plain to set off the ornament.

The enthusiasm of the Prince Regent, later George IV, for
shooting and collecting fine weapons was an encouragement
to English gunmakers to excel in their art. The superbly-
enriched guns of the period made for George IV, now in the
Royal Collection at Windsor Castle, bear testimony to their
excellence.

In the middle of the nineteenth century there was a fashion
in Europe for 'Gothic' decoration, especially in pairs of
duelling pistols or target pistols. The barrels, locks and furniture were elaborately chiselled in a type of ornament derived
largely from Gothic cathedrals. European sporting guns and
rifles were often enriched with deep engraving on the locks
and the carving of the stock with scenes of the chase.

In England, by contrast, ornament was restricted to simple
foliated scrolls which in no way detracted from the clean,
graceful and strictly functional shape of the gun. This tradition

A magnificent garniture of French Empire firearms: a rifle and pair of pistols by Nicholas-Noel Boutet, *c.* 1805. The silver mounts and inlay are superb examples of Empire period ornament. The barrels are blued and encrusted with gold at the breeches and muzzles and the space between is covered with a regular pattern of tiny inlaid gold stars. The graceful and efficient locks are engraved with restrained ornament. The weapons are contained in a fine velvet-lined fitted case with their equipment.

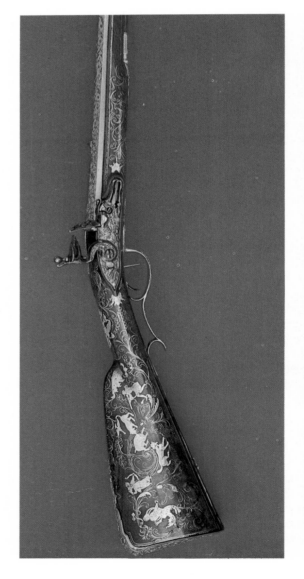

A very fine flintlock *Jäger* rifle made in Tula, Russia, for the Empress Elizabeth Petrovna, dated 1755. This rifle has richly chiselled ornament on the barrel and lock against a gold ground and heavily gilded bronze mounts. The walnut stock is inlaid with hunting scenes and scrolls in silver.

Far right: A magnificent pair of duelling pistols richly mounted in silver, hallmarked 1815. The mounts show classical subjects and trophies of arms. The locks and barrels are blued and inlaid with gold ornament. They were made by Brunn, London, for the Prince Regent, it is believed.

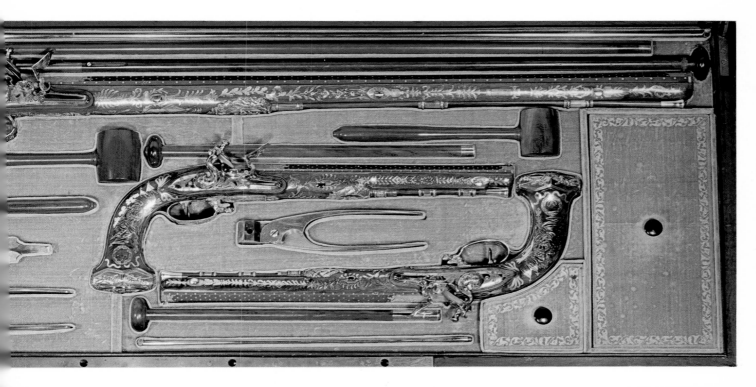

continued through the transition from muzzle-loading to breech-loading and has endured through the era of the modern hammerless ejector gun and rifle.

Having dealt briefly with some of the main trends in the decoration of guns in Europe, it should be appreciated that there were a number of areas that continued in their own way, largely unaffected by these developments.

Scotland provides a fascinating example of just such a national style for she produced guns and pistols of unique shape and a style of ornament which derived from the Celts. Seventeenth-century Scottish belt pistols were fitted with the Scottish version of the snaphance lock and had a wooden stock ending in what is usually described as a 'fish-tail' butt furnished with a metal butt-plate. Other distinctive features were the long belt-hook and the small baluster-shaped trigger without a guard. The lock and furniture were engraved with Celtic-style ornament. Other seventeenth-century pistols were of the all-metal type with a rounded octagonal-shaped pommel, the lock and metal stock being engraved with Celtic-style interlaced strapwork. The barrel and ramrod were often finished at the end with a turned baluster-shape.

The rare examples of seventeenth-century Scottish guns had snaphance locks and curious, curved and fluted butts with a notch for the thumb. Like the pistols, these guns usually have a baluster-shaped trigger.

In the late seventeenth and early eighteenth centuries, belt pistols were made entirely of metal, with flintlocks, a heart-shaped butt, and usually with a pricker (for cleaning the touch-hole) screwed into the end. The heart-shaped butt gave place to the typical eighteenth-century flat-sided butt, ending in the curled 'ram's horn' shape, with the pricker screwed in between the 'horns'. Scottish pistols usually have the barrel, lock and stock richly engraved with Celtic ornament, though some of them were engraved with foliated scrolls and inlaid with engraved silver plaques.

In the nineteenth century, richly-decorated pistols were made for wearing with highland costume during the Scottish Romantic movement.

To return to general trends, in recent years there has been a revival of the art of gun decoration in Europe, America and England. Once again fine sporting guns and rifles are being enriched with a variety of ornament, including deeply-engraved game scenes on the locks, on the trigger-guards and under the action. Alternatively the action body, locks and breech ends of the barrels are engraved, carved and further enriched with gold inlay. In some of the game scenes, animals such as elephant and lion on rifles and game birds on guns are inlaid in gold and carved in relief, giving a very rich effect. Some of the most superb work, comparable with the great traditions of the past, is being carried out by Kenneth Hunt in London today.

A Scottish all-steel belt pistol with a heart-shaped butt, by John Burgess of Elgin, *c.* 1700

A Scottish belt pistol with a flat-sided butt finished with 'ram's horn' curls and a pricker between them, by John Campbell of Doune, *c.* 1715. The engraving and silver inlay are in Celtic style.

A Scottish snaphance gun with its curious curved and fluted butt, dated 1685

Completed in 1971 by James Purdey & Sons, London, this gun has been superbly decorated in gold by Ken Hunt. The Renaissance style scrollwork is inlaid flush and shaded with engraving. The pheasants and pointer on the right lock plate and the squirrels and oak branches behind the breech are carved semi-round. Three bob-white quail are inlaid on the trigger-guard and a carving of the head of Pan in gold forms the finiel of the beaver-tail forend.

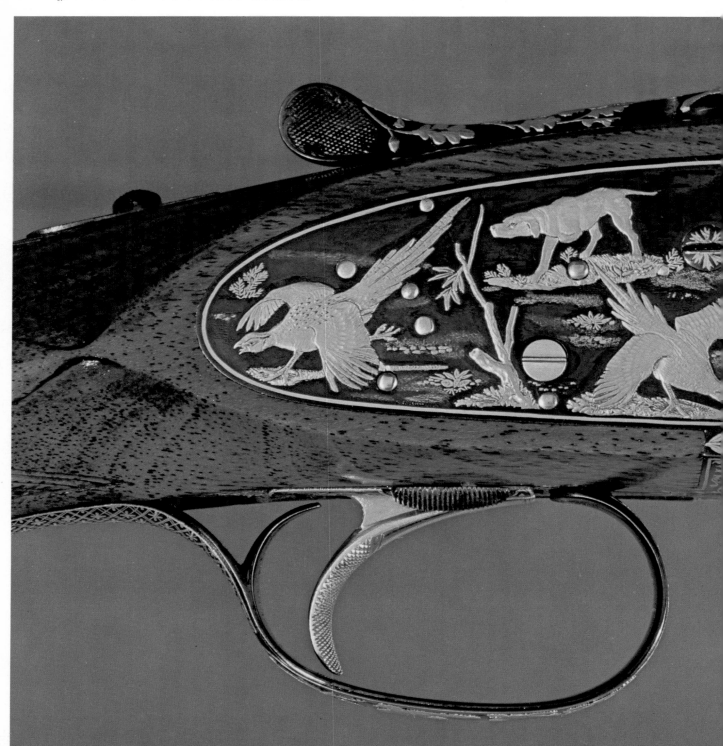

Index

Acknowledgments

Photographs are reproduced by courtesy of the following :-
Australian News & Information Bureau 103 bottom
Author 11 top, 47, 58–59, 65, 91 bottom
Trustees of The British Museum contents page
Amon Carter Museum, Fort Worth, Texas 81 top
Christie, Manson & Woods, London 85, 112 top and
bottom, 113 top and bottom, 116–117, 118–119 top
Churchill Ltd., London 68–69 top
Fabrique Nationale, Herstal 105 top and upper centre
Richard Green Gallery, London 42–43
Imperial War Museum, London 36 top and bottom, 37 top
Kungl. Livrustkammaren, Stockholm end-papers, half-title,
jacket flaps, 110 bottom, 111 bottom
National Army Museum, Chelsea 18 top, 19 top, 23
bottom, 26–27, 30–31 bottom, 31 top, 34, 35, 68–69
bottom
W. Keith Neal Collection front and back jacket, 6, 7 top,
centre and bottom, 10, 14 top, centre and bottom, 15 top,
16, 17 top, 21 bottom, 38, 39 top, 40, 41, 43 top and
bottom, 44, 45 left and right, 46 top and bottom, 48 top
and bottom, 49, 50, 54 top, 63 top and bottom, 66, 82–83,
83 right, 84, 86, 90, 92, 93, 94, 94–95, 96 top and bottom,
100–101 top and centre, 102, 114 right, 115, 118 bottom,
120–121 top, centre and bottom
Diana Keith Neal Collection 98
James Purdey and Sons Ltd., London 51 bottom, 53,
122–123
Remington Art Museum, Ogdensburg, New York 73 right
Royal Military Academy Sandhurst 18–19 bottom
Shooting Times and Country Magazine, Maidenhead
59 right
Sotheby and Co., London 89, 100–101 bottom
Tower of London (crown copyright reserved) title page, 15
centre and bottom, 17 bottom, 21 top, 24, 32 top, 33, 71
centre and right
Union Pacific Railroad Museum Collection 78–79
Victoria and Albert Museum 22–23 top, 62 (crown
copyright reserved), 106–107 bottom, 114 left
Wallace Collection, London 106–107 top, 108–109 top,
110–111 top
Webley and Scott Ltd., Birmingham 61
Winchester Gun Museum, New Haven, Connecticut
72–73 top, centre and bottom, 74 left, 74–75 top, 76–77
centre and bottom, 80–81, 81 bottom

Sources of photographs :-
Geoffrey Boothroyd 105 lower centre and bottom
Harriet Bridgeman Ltd., London title page
Bulloz, Paris 29 bottom
Amon Carter Museum, Fort Worth, Texas 81 top
Central Office of Information, London 37 (crown
copyright reserved)
Christie, Manson and Woods, London 85, 112 top and
bottom, 113 top and bottom, 116–117, 118–119 top
Churchill Ltd., London 68–69 top
Department of the Environment (crown copyright
reserved) 15 centre and bottom, 17 bottom, 21 top, 24,
32 top, 33, 72 centre and right
Mary Evans Picture Library, London 80 top
Fabrique Nationale, Herstal 105 top and upper centre
Richard Green Gallery, London 42–43
Hamlyn Group Picture Library C. Crosthwaite: 11 centre
and bottom, 25 top and bottom, 54 bottom, 56–57, 57 top,
58 top; J. R. Freeman and Co. Ltd.: contents page;
Hawkley Studios: 18–19, 51 bottom, 53, 114 left, 122–123;
W. Keith Neal: front and back jacket, 6, 7 top, centre and
bottom, 10, 14 top centre and bottom, 15 top, 16, 17 top,
21 bottom, 38, 39 top, 40, 41, 43 top and bottom, 44, 45
left and right, 46 top and bottom, 48 top and bottom, 49,
50, 54 top, 63 top and bottom, 66, 82–83, 83 right, 84, 86,
90, 92, 93, 94, 94–95, 96 top and bottom, 98, 100–101 top
and centre, 102, 114 right, 115, 118 bottom, 120–121 top
centre and bottom
Imperial War Museum, London 36 top and bottom, 37 top
Kungl. Livrustkammaren, Stockholm end-papers, half-
title, jacket flaps, 110 bottom, 111 bottom
Mansell Collection, London 13, 32 bottom, 35 bottom, 51
top, 87, 91 top, 103 top, 104–105
National Army Museum, Chelsea 18 top, 19 top, 23
bottom, 26–27, 30–31 bottom, 31 top, 34, 35 top, 68–69
bottom
Radio Times Hulton Picture Library 29 top, 67, 68 left,
70–71, 97
Remington Art Museum, Ogdensburg, New York 73 right
Shooting Times and Country Magazine, Maidenhead 59
right
Sotheby and Co., London 89, 100–101 bottom
Union Pacific Railroad Museum Collection 78–79
Victoria and Albert Museum, London 22–23 top, 62
(crown copyright reserved), 106–107 bottom
Wallace Collection, London 106–107 top, 108–109 top,
110–111 top
Webley and Scott Ltd., Birmingham 61
Winchester Gun Museum, New Haven, Connecticut 72–73
top, centre and bottom, 74 left, 74–75 top, 76–77 centre,
76–77 bottom, 80–81, 81 bottom